WALKING THE
PRECIPICE

WALKING THE PRECIPICE

Witness to the Rise of the Taliban in Afghanistan

Barbara Bick

Foreword by Eden Naby

The Feminist Press
at the City University of New York
New York

Published in 2009 by The Feminist Press at The City University of New York
The Graduate Center
365 Fifth Avenue, Suite 5406
New York, NY 10016
www.feministpress.org

Library of Congress Cataloging-in-Publication Data
Bick, Barbara.
Walking the Precipice : Witness to the Rise of the Taliban / Barbara Bick; Foreword by
Eden Naby. — 1st ed.
p. cm.
Includes bibliographical references.
ISBN-13: 978-1-55861-586-1 (pbk. : alk. paper)
ISBN-13: 978-1-55861-592-2 (library : alk. paper)

1. Afghanistan—History—1990-2003. 2. Afghanistan—History—1990-2003. Taliban.
4. Bick, Barbara. I. Title.
DS371.3.B53 2009
958.104'6—dc22
2008009274

13 12 11 10 09 5 4 3 2 1

For the two most important women in my life

My mother, Moma Lil
LILLIAN COLODNY LICHTENSTEIN: a wise, beautiful woman
whose activist life was circumscribed by societal parameters

My daughter, Kathy
KATHRINE BICK: brilliant, insatiable reader, loving woman
whose life was tragically distorted by mental illness

CONTENTS

FOREWORD

Western women who venture into Afghanistan with the expectation of conducting research, interviews, or otherwise investigating political or social situations, must inevitably negotiate the gender issue. As a young United States Peace Corps volunteer in Mazar-i-Sharif during the 1960s, my concession to the near total social segregation of women was a headscarf and modest clothing. But the true toll of a segregated society was the feelings of boredom, isolation, and loneliness that I, along with my Western and Afghan friends, experienced. The social and intellectual lives of Afghan women, even in a major city like Mazar, were meager, entwined mainly with household chores, children, husbands, and other wives.

Not much has improved for Afghan women until very recently. The three trips that Barbara Bick documents here in a personal and highly engaging way contain significant indicators that change is coming about for all Afghan women during the post-9/11 era. Although the security situation remains fragile, and women's education, employment, and basic human rights are threatened with each success of the resurgent Taliban, the determination of so many Afghan women to reconceive the future for their children, their country, and themselves offers hope for several reasons.

Now that they have tasted relative emancipation after five

years of Taliban control, women will not easily be shoved back into the oblivion of the burqa again. Nor will Afghan women take for granted the rights they have won, claimed especially through widely circulated declarations of women's rights and the mobilization for the Loya Jirga in 2003. These rights expand upon those previously granted during the 1960s by a liberalizing monarchy and, as Bick witnessed during her 1990 visit, by the Communist government of Najibullah. They build upon a history of women's rights in Afghanistan that the Taliban and other fundamentalists have historically ignored.

Even more important, women in Afghanistan's cities recognize the necessity of bridging the chasm that exists between urban elites and their sisters in the countryside. We will have to wait to see how far into eastern and southern Afghanistan this women's awakening has reached, but it is possible to measure it through statistics on women's literacy programs, girl's schooling facilities, and the evidence that some of the strictures imposed by Pashtun tradition—which weighs heavily upon most of Afghanistan's nearly thirty-two million people, women and men alike—are being lifted. Afghan women's organizations that were created in refugee situations and in Western diaspora are now an established fact of Afghan life, even if their existence in all parts of the home country may at times appear tenuous.

The current erosion of political stability in Afghanistan began in the 1970s with the simultaneous end of the monarchial system, the rise of ethnic politics, the coalescing of communist movements, and the emergence of Islamist politics. Ten odd years of mujahidin resistance to the Soviet invasion, the subsequent imposition in Kabul of rural gender attitudes by the quarreling mujahidin parties that replaced the Soviet-backed regime, and the ensuing misogynistic rule of the Taliban sent the cause of women's rights and human rights back into medieval times.

Barbara Bick's memoirs cover a substantial part of this period of great change. She opens windows on Afghan women negotiating the shifting political scene in 1990, 2001, and 2003. The span of these thirteen years represents a time of extended civil war that was complicated by ethnic and sectarian animosity. Bick saw the Kabul-based end of Soviet-style social engineering, with its tableaus of women's progress. During her trip to northern Afghanistan in August 2001 she witnessed the efforts of the opposition to create an antidote to the gendered cruelty of the Taliban regime. And finally, in 2003, she was an observer at a conference organized by Afghan women to build support for incorporating women's rights into the country's constitution, a document that spells policy in Afghanistan today although implementation is another matter. But, as Bick's descriptions of her 2001 visit to the Northern Alliance-controlled region show, a defeat on the battlefield could easily mean a political reversal that drives all women under the burqa. Women's rights are fragile in Afghanistan, shallowly rooted in society, and progress is susceptible to setback with an assassin's bullet.

Bick was witness to the recent impact of Islamists who dream of transforming Afghanistan into a Caliphate that will re-create the glory of Islam's eighth century dominance. This dream was first expressed in the twentieth century when the rise of Soviet communism sent Muslim refugees out of Central Asia into Afghanistan, the Indian sub-continent, Turkey, and Saudi Arabia. It remains alive among fundamentalist Muslims living in the mountains that spill between Afghanistan and Pakistan, where the Pashtun tribes (and their Al Qaeda guests) remain virtually immune to central government rule. The key to this dream has been, and is again, control of Afghanistan. The country has come to symbolize the one place in the Muslim world that has not been colonized, whose customs have not been tainted by Tsarist Russian, British, French, or other forms of nineteenth century imperialist rule.

Today the struggle in Afghanistan attracts ethnic fighters from Chechnya to Xinjiang. A major symbol of the dream of reestablishing the Caliphate revolves around the suppression of women, or, as these Muslim fighters and their strategists would regard it, upholding the honor of Muslim men.

Much has been written about the role of the United States in supporting the mujahidin factions that spawned the Taliban. Some ten years before Bick's first visit to Afghanistan, in late February 1980, I arranged for a CBS 60 Minutes production team, with anchor Dan Rather, to enter Afghanistan guided by a group of mujahidin. I accompanied the team, serving as a translator. That trip marked the first successful Western TV attempt to enter Afghanistan under Soviet occupation. It was a scene from the resulting 60 Minutes episode, aired in March 1980, that apparently inspired Congressman Charlie Wilson (D–Tex.) to offer US aid to the mujahidin.

In the course of making the documentary, we interviewed the major mujahidin groups who were then headquartered or represented in Pakistan. Roughly speaking, these groups divided along ethnic and political lines. Pashtuns formed the majority of the resistance parties not only because their ethnic group straddles the Afghan-Pakistani border and their flight to refuge was shorter than for others, but also because as the rulers of Afghanistan since its establishment in the eighteenth century, they were eager to renew their political power.

We also met with Tajiks, who represent the second largest group in Afghanistan. The Tajiks' position north of the Hindu Kush mountains allowed them to harass the Soviet military supply lines during the period of Soviet invasion. Several smaller Dari-Persian speaking ethnic groups and some Turkic ones were allied with them, and still are today. All these groups are Sunni, leaving the Shia Hazara quite isolated and without allies in the country, and only Shiite Iran concerned about their interests outside the country. The Tajiks and their allies, though politically powerful, were confined to one party, led by Burhanuddin Rabbani, who was the president of a truncated Afghanistan at the time Barbara Bick made her second visit in 2001.

Crosscutting this ethnic divide were Islamist elements, more radical among the Pashtuns than among the Tajiks. The fieriest among these was Gulbuddin Hekmatyar, a man whose following included many Pashtuns living on the Pakistani side of the border. The Pashtun political parties also included that of Pir Sayed Ahmad Gailani, a more tolerant Sufi religious leader and one of the urban elite. His faction, secular in nature, was most concerned with modernizing Afghanistan along a constitutional track, but it was estranged from the Pashtun and Tajik countryside.

The natural course of political sympathies might have led the US to back Pir Gailani, but there were tactical reasons for not choosing that path: Gailani had hardly any fighters in Afghanistan, and his demand for the restoration of an independent Afghanistan meant his group had no friends among the Pakistani elite advising the US. Ironically, the US and NATO have been trying desperately to build alliances with liberal groups such as his since 2003. It is in this context that the US and its allies, the United Nations, and independent nongovernmental organizations (NGOs) have come to support an expanded role for women, while the Taliban, in its southern stronghold, seeks to restrict women's opportunities by bombing schools and killing teachers.

Dependent on Pakistan for access to land-locked Afghanistan, and convinced that successful resistance to the Soviet military lay in supporting Islamist groups, the US made alliances with mujahidin linked to deeply conservative Wahhabi forces in the Gulf, who were also supporting fundamentalists in Pakistan. As the US became more drawn into supporting radical Muslims as a bulwark against communism, it found itself arming and financing radical parties that despised the West as intensely as they hated the "godless" Soviet Union.

In the refugee camps sheltering four to five million Afghans, run by Pashtun fundamentalist groups, the suppression of women grew alarmingly throughout the 1980s. The elites and

the educated escaped the stifling political atmosphere of Peshawar for other urban centers in India and Pakistan, and eventually made their way to the US, Australia, and Europe. President
Hamid Karzai and many of the Afghans who made Barbara
Bick's third visit to Kabul in 2003 so interesting and hospitable,
come from this secularized, mainly Pashtun urban group that
has endeavored to re-introduce constitutional democratic values
into Afghan society.[1] The majority of Pashtuns, like other isolated and rural tribal people, continued to hold to their customs
with tenacity.

Among Pashtuns, the basis for law lies in the Koran, the
Hadith (traditions recounted by the companions of the proph-
et), local custom, and analogy. Local custom is the unforgiving
Pashtunwali, tribal code that trumps the Sunni school of law
followed officially in Afghanistan, the relatively liberal Hanafi
Shari'a. The pro-Soviet Kabul regime led by President Najibullah, whom Barbara Bick's delegation met in 1990, did not succeed in enforcing laws that countered the Pashtunwali, nor did
previous liberal Afghan governments, and the Taliban made
significant aspects of this code the law of the land, especially
with regard to its harsh dictates on women.

As a woman interpreting Afghan culture to male representatives of the Western media in 1980, I felt the weight of Pashtun rural attitudes toward me as a female. I was the first
non-Soviet foreign woman to enter Afghanistan after the invasion. With women such a rarity among those writing about the
situation, even the KGB assumed that Eden was the name of a
man. In fact, Western women often have difficulty functioning
in rural Pashtun settings. In 2008, women aid workers are killed
in Pashtun areas not only because the resurgent Taliban have
allies there but because Pashtun men in the villages have no
scale by which to assess women's position except that of their
customary codes, which circumscribe women's role within the
strict physical confines of the family home.

Several times in this narrative, Barbara Bick reiterates that her age (sixty-five on her first trip) allowed her more freedom of movement, within limits, than would have been permitted to a younger woman. I, on the other hand, was a young woman traveling in the company of four Western men and half a dozen Pashtun mujahidin. For the Afghans with whom I had to interact, my presence was problematic.

Thrown off by having to deal through a woman with media representatives whom they hoped to engage in their struggle, the mujahidin we traveled with adopted two tactics. Some of them, once over their reluctance to address a foreign unveiled woman, treated me like a sister, climbing trails without waiting for me, giving me privacy, asking for advice about contraception to reduce the responsibility of having more mouths to feed, and attempting to convert me to Islam in the course of long hikes along goat paths. But some Afghan men, especially those whose language I did not know, attempted crude physical insults.

I refused to wear the burqa, even though Gulbuddin Hekmatyar's assistants insisted I do so for an interview. Hekmatyar, an ally of the Taliban, lived to see that oppressive, pleated bag become mandatory for all women under the Taliban. To protect my hair from dust, and as a concession to Afghan custom, I sometimes wore a white scarf, although because it was easy to spot from Soviet helicopters, I would often remove it quickly. The burqa is not only a symbol of women's suppression; many Afghan men fleeing from one or another conflict have been willing to use it to escape through lines where women are allowed to pass untouched. But for women forced to view the world through its embroidered web, it is akin to a shroud.

Among Bick's most vivid descriptions are the scenes of women's gatherings, whether for political discussions or for dinner in private homes. She notes the various ways in which women in different age categories deal with unveiling: some throw back the burqa to reveal their face and hair, others lift it over their face but keep their hair covered, while many younger women simply wear white or colorful scarves. Others make a point of not covering their hair, sporting nail polish, and wearing Western suits. It is clear that individual women operate at their specific comfort level, which has notably increased in recent years, allowing greater self-expression in terms of segregation and veiling.

What is this obsession with covering women in Afghan society? In place of a satisfactory answer, I recall the tormented elderly Afghan man running toward our CBS crew, shouting in Pashtu-accented Dari. We were searching through a teeming camp outside Peshawar for images to convey the terrible life of the refugees who had fled their villages in advance of the Soviet army during the winter of 1980. The producer wanted poignant images, which should include women and children. With tents pitched within five or six feet of each other, the camp we visited offered little privacy for families. Women were confined even more than at home since they did not have a family compound in which to move around.

The gaunt elderly man, running frantically, was pleading and threatening at the same time: "They have taken everything from us! Do not take away our honor! Do not take pictures of our women!" According to the Pashtunwali, honor lies in the seclusion of women, and in punishing those whose chastity has been infringed upon, no matter what the cause.

We retreated. And that first electrifying visual account of the Soviet invasion of Afghanistan that propelled Congressman Charlie Wilson to crusade for Afghan aid became almost exclusively a political and military documentary. As a woman, I had been invited into the stifling refugee tents to sit with the thin and unkempt women and children. I offered them sympathy and candy. But no men were allowed in, and we were not allowed to film the women.

As the bravery and dedication of women like Mary MacMakin and her Afghan colleagues demonstrates in this book, the expansion of girls' schools and adult literacy into the countryside promises to enliven and expand Afghan women's lives.

But very little can change without efforts to promote reproductive rights. Afghanistan has the seventh highest fertility rate in the world, which is linked to the enormous effect of confining women; under Taliban control, the country's birth rate grew even more.

Women are often the touchstone for efforts to move many world cultures away from old patterns of social behavior. As such, Afghan women have been the ideological battleground for the better part of the twentieth century: How should they dress? Where can they work? When and whom can they marry? Who can they speak to or be with? Afghan society has insisted on determining the answers to such questions, more often than not, without consultation with women, just as similar questions have been answered throughout the world until recent centuries. Under Taliban rule the condition of women became particularly difficult. As with tribal societies like the Kurds of Turkey and Iraq, the Pashtuns adapted Islam as a mantle covering local tribal customs in which woman are indicators of wealth and position and, of course, the vessel for continuity of a male line of descent.

Due to the window that women offer into Afghan social history, anthropologists in particular have explored women's issues at specific locations, concentrating on regions representing one or another of the many ethnic pockets of the country. But most areas have not been accessible to women scholars. And it is hardly surprising that male scholars from any country have had little access to Afghan women for research purposes. In most histories and political studies, there are only passing references to key events such as the start of women's schools, official unveiling of Afghan women, and women in political life.

This is one of the reasons that Barbara Bick's memoir is so important; it brings together a number of strands in Afghan women's studies. On her first trip, Bick, a long time feminist activist, was confined to Kabul in the company of another feminist with a strident pro-Soviet political agenda. During her second trip she traveled with staunchly anti-communist Nasrine Gross, a member of the pre-Soviet Kabul elite, an Afghan American woman of recognized dedication, education, and wit, whose concerns are for Afghan women and Afghanistan. Bick's memoirs run smoothly through the valley between the extremist ideologies of the right and the left. She achieves this feat by providing background about her own political activism while at the same time demonstrating respect for the dedication of Afghan women activists and Western women who come from a more rightist position. In fact, Bick's commentary proves through many examples that the situation of Afghan women has been so oppressive that Western observers, both on the right and the left, are almost certain to agree that international aid must be directed to Afghan women and girls, most specifically in the area of education, but also in terms of their employment opportunities and legal improvement of status overall.

As with much social progress in the developing world, the basic work of improving Afghan women's situation must be done at the grassroots, rural level. Tribute must be given to the dozens of dedicated Afghan women, some now assassinated, who were and are the ones capable of sustained effort on behalf of women in the countryside. Western feminists must support Afghan women, document and publicize their work, and encourage them to spread children's education throughout the country in a manner that breaks the customary pattern of boys raised to discriminate against girls in their own homes and in society.

This book shows how Afghan women from the diaspora are coming together with local women to draft and implement such groundbreaking ideas as those expressed in the Declaration of the Essential Rights of Afghan Women (appearing at the end of this book). If one is interested in the peaceful transition of our small world toward a future of promise for all, the danger of allowing the conventional role of Afghan women, particularly as defined by the Pashtunwali, to continue ought to encourage even the least political among us to take an interest in the position of Afghan women.

1. Naby, Eden. "The Afghan Diaspora: Reflections on an Imagined Country," in *Central Asia and the Caucasus: Transnationalism and Diaspora*, eds. S. Mehendale and T. Atabaki (New York: Routledge, 2005).

PREFACE

From somewhere, I watch. I see an elderly American woman hunched on a thin pallet on the dirt floor of a mud-brick and woven-reed hut. Her eyes are dulled with grief and exhaustion. She looks across the small, bare room toward her companion. A kerosene lantern on the floor flickers near the single opening into the hut. The two women are silent.

A burly, bearded Afghan enters the room. It is his hut. A frail Uzbek boy follows, his bone-thin arms quivering under the weight of a large tray of kabobs, nan, watermelon, and grapes. He lays the tray on the reed mat that covers the earthen floor. I see the older woman close her eyes and lie down. I feel her dry throat, know she cannot eat. My muscles tighten as she shifts her body awkwardly on the hard ground and groans. Her eyes closed, she listens to the drone of unintelligible voices as her friend and the man eat and converse in Dari.

It is the evening of September 9, 2001, in a far northern outpost in Afghanistan. The older woman is me, but I am also somewhere outside myself that night. Hours earlier, in the compound where my companion and I were staying, Al Qaeda terrorists had murdered a top commander of the Northern Alliance, the only group of Afghans fighting the Taliban. The compound was mad with grief, and perhaps with something else as well—fear and despair. As for me, what has led me to this unlikely place—and will I leave it alive? These thoughts drift through my mind as I shift around, half asleep, trying to fit my arthritic body into the hollows of the dirt floor. When the man leaves, I push myself up. It takes all my strength. "Nasrine," I say to my companion, who is leaning against the wall of the hut, smoking, "please take my picture."

"Later, later," she says impatiently.

I can only guess what she thinks of my request. Perhaps she considers it narcissistic, or absurdly American. But I have an urgent, almost desperate need to make this moment real. I awkwardly, painfully get to my feet and totter over to her with the camera. "Please, Nasrine, take my picture."

Back on my pallet, I slump, exhausted, against the wall. The flash brightens the room momentarily. I sink back down, satisfied that when this is over, the photograph will bear witness.

Chapter 1
Kabul, 1990

My first trip to Afghanistan is in 1990, the year I turn sixty-five. College, during World War II, then marriage and young children had been obstacles to my abiding desire to travel. It was not until my early forties that I became a traveler and then it was most often because of my work in the women's peace movement. As a representative of Women Strike for Peace to international conferences, I often found myself in countries with political systems inimical to the United States, such as Cuba and the Soviet Union, and worked on committees with women and men who had diverse agendas, and from them I learned something about the real lives of people beyond my own Western world. When I travel I am fascinated by regions with ancient, non-Western cultures and alternate political systems where I can see and hopefully better understand the lives of the people who live there. As a feminist, I am always especially interested in the conditions under which other women live.

After my divorce and with my three children grown, I traveled more frequently, most often alone and away from beaten paths. I lived for a year in Europe, to feel the beat of life in a region far older than America. I picked Italy for its history—and cuisine—and the nontourist city of Bologna, governed by the Italian Communist Party.

And then in 1990, having just reached the threshold of senior status, I began to think about one last, unforgettable journey before "old age" kicked in. Fortuitously, several months after my birthday, at a noisy reception in Washington, D.C., I met a woman I knew slightly from my years of work in the peace movement.

Rather abruptly, Gabi comes up to me and says that she and another woman I also barely know are going to Afghanistan on an invitation from the women's peace movement there. Would I like to join them?

My first trip to Afghanistan begins as simply as that.

Gabi is a tiny, vivid Italian American and a tireless activist. Unlike Cynthia, the other woman who will be on the trip, and who is a nurse and a true do-gooder, always ready to defend those in need, Gabi is utterly ideological, an anachronism in the peace community. Despite the fact that most progressives had given up on the Soviet Union decades earlier, Gabi rigorously defends all of the USSR's—and now Russia's—actions. Thus, her only interest in Afghanistan has been triggered by the 1979 Soviet invasion. I do not agree with her politically, but I sense no political requirements on my side, and it seems an ideal opportunity to participate with these two women in a fascinating trip to an unknown part of the world. And that is good enough for me. Afghanistan seems just right for the kind of slightly adventurous experience I am looking for.

I know, of course, that there has been a war, but it appears to have ended with the Russian withdrawal the previous year. Other than that, I realize, I am clueless and so go on a crash course to learn more about the country and its political history before I leave. I learn that for nearly a decade, Soviet troops have fought a bloody and vastly demoralizing (for the Soviets) war, ostensibly to help their fellow Communists in Afghanistan. After the Soviets left, the Afghan Communist government managed to hold on to power. As we prepare for our journey, they still control the government in Kabul with their own armed forces, and I assume that the city and surrounding areas are relatively safe.

Since the US government refuses to recognize the government, there is no exchange of ambassadors between the two countries. Afghanistan's US embassy maintains a skeleton crew, headed by a chargé d'affaires, thirty-eight-year-old Miagol (like many Afghans, he has only one name). Through his efforts, Gabi has obtained this invitation for an American women's delegation to visit the country.

Before we leave, Miagol invites the three of us for dinner at the embassy. It is a simple family meal with his wife, Sima, and their two young children. During dinner, Miagol tells us that he is "tremendously moved" by his experience in the United States. "Before living in Washington," he says, "I knew only that Americans were greedy capitalists and thought only of money. The free museums, the free parks astonished me—and free water for people to drink! I love to be in Washington," he enthuses, "and to play soccer in the Adams Morgan Park."

We discuss the situation in Afghanistan, and he contradicts Gabi when she says the Soviets had not invaded, but had only come in response to a call for help by the faltering Afghan Communists. "That is just part of the truth," he insists. "Friends come with peace corps, not with armies and bombs. The mujahidin are also Afghans, and for many Afghans, we, the government, are not the 'good guys.'"

I listen closely. What exactly are *mujahidin*? And why do they oppose the government Miagol represents? I realize that I am going into a complicated situation about which I still understand little.

Miagol tells us that mujahidin is the Muslim word for "holy warriors," fighters for God. He explains that the vast majority of Afghan people are very poor peasants who live in small villages. Ninety percent are illiterate. They are deeply religious and get much of their information from local mullahs, Islamic clergy, some of whom are themselves uneducated, and many of whom hold extreme fundamentalist views. The literate 10 percent of Afghans live mostly in towns and cities, and the most educated, professional Afghans almost all live in the capital city of Kabul. Many among these elites form the leadership of the Communist Party, the People's Democratic Party of Afghanistan (PDPA).

Miagol says that although they are also Muslims, PDPA members favor a modern secular state, which places them in opposition to the mullahs, and to a majority of rural Afghans. That opposition only intensified when the PDPA welcomed the "godless" Soviets into Afghanistan. The mujahidin have fought a long guerrilla war against these atheists; and now, after defeating the Russians, they are still at war with their own Communists. To the mujahidin and their supporters, Miagol reiterates, the Communists who rule the country could never be the good guys.

"Oh, Miagol," Gabi tweaks him, "you've been out of the country too long." I am annoyed that she would challenge an Afghan official, who certainly knows more about his own country than she does. But I am very interested by what he says next: "If I were twenty years old I would remain in the US." But he isn't twenty, and he is, in fact, being recalled to Afghanistan. His wife and children, who also want to stay in the United States, will go to her parents, who live in the Ukraine. "It is too dangerous in Kabul," he says sadly. There is a sort of civil war going on, he admits, but adds that the capital is under total government control and for some time will remain relatively safe for visitors like us.

I feel a twinge of fear.

As our departure date approaches, I develop more qualms, then moments of panic, and even begin to wonder whether I will be able to tolerate my companions' politics. But I deeply want this last adventure and feel reassured by Miagol's support of the trip and the fact that we are being sponsored by a women's organization.

So, despite my ambivalent feelings, I head to the doctor for all the necessary shots and summarily dismiss the cautions of family and friends against going.

Gabi, Cynthia, and I leave Washington in the middle of summer for India, where we board a plane for Kabul. As I look down from the plane on an enormous desert, crimson hills, and stark cliffs, I am enthralled. My spirits lighten. Legendary names echo in my brain.

I am seeing the terrain over which Alexander the Great passed in the third century B.C., after he defeated the great Persian empire of Darius III. Alexander's army, in subzero weather, crossed the Hindu Kush, the majestic mountain range of eastern Afghanistan, whose highest peaks reach altitudes of seventeen thousand feet. Alexander founded many cities in the region, some of which flourished, were destroyed, were rebuilt, and are once again vibrant today. And Alexander's army was only the first. The snow-covered mountains are cut through by passes, which, over more than two thousand years, became well-forged routes through which armies, traders, religions, cultures, and people penetrated and permeated Afghanistan. In the seventh century, Islamic Arabs conquered and converted the people of the region.

The Mongol chief Genghis Khan, his conquests eclipsing Alexander's, overrode this vast quarter of the earth in 1219. Peter Hopkirk's book *The Great Game* describes the Mongol warriors thus: "You could smell them coming even before you heard the thunder of their hooves. But by then it was too late. Within seconds came the first murderous torrent of arrows, blotting out the sun and turning day into night. Like molten lava, they destroyed everything in their path [leaving] a trail of smoking cities and bleached bones."

Kublai Khan, grandson of Genghis, founded the Mongol dynasty in China, and his uncles and cousins built Mongol empires that encompassed Hungary, Syria, Persia, Tibet, northern India, the Caucasus, and all of Central Asia, including

Afghanistan. With my face pressed against the plane's window, I strain to resurrect the vanished masses of Mongols, their flashing scimitars and galloping horses. Tamerlane and Babur also traversed Afghanistan for the purpose of extending their empires and left a heritage of superb architecture and culture. Zoroastrians, Buddhists, Hindus, and Jews all set up colonies. People from the four cultures that surround Afghanistan—Indian, Persian, Chinese, and Central Asian—left their imprint on the land and the people.

All these influences are part of Afghan culture now. But modern Afghanistan is comprised primarily of four groups. The Pashtuns, the largest of the ethnic groups, speak Pashto and predominate in the south and east of the country, next to Pakistan. Tajiks, the second-largest group, primarily reside in the north and northeast. Turkic groups, including Uzbeks, Turkmen, and Kazakhs, dominate in the northwest, while Hazaras, the only Afghans with Mongol physical characteristics, reside in the center and west. The last three groups speak Dari, an Afghan version of Persian, as their first or second language; this is the lingua franca of Afghanistan, but there are many local dialects. Most Afghans are Muslim, split between the majority Sunni sect and the Shia. For much of its history, Afghanistan tolerated religious diversity. Hindus, Sikhs, and Jews played a significant role in the country's economy. Proselytizing was forbidden, so Christian communities were scarce.

In the early eighteenth century, a Pashtun warrior, Ahmed Shah, united many of the Afghan clans to form the Durrani Empire, one of the most powerful Islamic empires of all time. After his death, the country slipped into civil war. Victorian Britain and czarist Russia, eyeing a potentially valuable prize, vied for control in what came to be known as "the Great Game." Britain invaded three times in the 1800s, attempting to create a buffer state between Russia and Britain's "jewel in the crown," India.

Afghanistan took control of its destiny again in the twentieth century, and in 1919 a new king, Amanullah Khan, came to power determined to bring in Western ideas about government. To my mind, he is one of the most exciting as well as one of the most tragic rulers in Afghan history. Inspired by Mustafa Kemal Atatürk's reforms in Turkey, he rushed into creating a civil legal code and a legislative assembly, and advocated reforms such as the emancipation of women and universal education. Atatürk had warned Amanullah to go slowly, good advice that went unheeded. Powerful religious leaders became hostile to Amanullah, claiming that the king had "turned against Allah and Islam!" Proof of this included pictures of Amanullah's wife, Queen Soraya, appearing unveiled at receptions in European capitals.

After ruling for ten years, Amanullah was forced into exile and Afghan society reverted to tribal, authoritarian, and patriarchal mores. Arnold Hunter, an American journalist who spent much of his life in Asia, was shocked by what he viewed as the backwardness of Afghanistan and saw, even then, that its treatment of women was symbolic of the ways in which fundamentalist traditions crippled the nation: "The fundamental problem of Afghanistan was that of their women," he wrote in the 1950s, "the basic issue on which all others hinged. Only by seeing it at first hand, was I able to appreciate how the status of women struck deeply into the roots of Afghan society, strangling and choking minds and bodies. The sight of so many of these formless, wraith-like figures slithering along the thoroughfare like carriers of some dreadful plague has to be seen for its full malignant effect to be truly grasped. It was heart sickening."

Fundamentalists of the twentieth and twenty-first centuries seem to have learned a jarring political lesson from that historic period: Maintaining oppressive gender roles is one of the most potent weapons in opposing modernity.

In the 1960s, another king made an attempt to democratize Afghanistan and to once again encourage women's participation in the public sphere. Mohammed Zahir Shah—who had become shah (king) all the way back in 1933 but ceded power to his paternal uncles—took over as an independent ruler in 1963. Zahir Shah was able to introduce a new democratic constitution in 1964 that formalized free elections, parliament, civil rights, women's liberation, and universal suffrage. Ten years of relative stability followed during which the country began to open up again to the rest of the world. However, political dissent against libralism was a powerful force; Zahir Shah was accused of corruption and deposed in a coup led by his cousin Mohammed Daoud Khan (who was overthrown in his turn by the Communists who seized power in 1978).

During this time, the Cold War continued to intensify and a new Great Game developed between the two most powerful twentieth-century empires, the United States and the Soviet Union. And Afghanistan was once again the playing field. The Soviet government invaded in 1979 while the United States chose covert intervention.

Now I was about to land in this deeply traditional and religious country that was emerging from a fierce ten-year battle against an occupying army, a country that was now apparently mired in a civil war.

Proof that there is reason to be concerned about safety comes when we are told not to worry about the landing, since Afghan pilots have perfected a spiral-descent tactic that avoids the missiles the mujahidin are hurling at the city! We hold our collective breath as the plane begins its twirling descent into Kabul and lands without incident. At the small, empty airport, several international aid workers are astonished to come across three Americans. We are, indeed, rare visitors.

Zahera and Shakira, two women from the All-Afghan Women's Council that is hosting us, greet us and drive us downtown to the three-story Hotel Kabul. We travel through a city that shows little damage from the war. A settlement for some twenty-five hundred years in the Kabul River valley, it is situated at an elevation of six thousand feet, lying in a bowl encircled by the treeless foothills of the Hindu Kush range. The city's beautiful setting is also eminently strategic: it is key to the Khyber Pass and, potentially, control of the Indian subcontinent. The city was spared wholesale destruction during the war, as both the Soviets and the Communist government needed it in order to control the country.

Zahera and Shakira are apologetic that we are not staying at Kabul's luxury hotel, the Continental, situated on one of the hills surrounding the city like a necklace. But it is safer in town. We are told that we cannot leave the hotel without an escort and that we will not see any of the country outside Kabul. They justify the limits of our trip by explaining that the city is swollen with people fleeing from devastated villages, that the borders with Pakistan and Iran are "porous," and that yes, as we have been told, the mujahidin are still battling the government. We are devastated. We had imagined we would be able to travel outside the city and be on our own once in a while.

With many apologies, the two women leave us, and we head down to dinner in the hotel's gloomy, cavernous, and nearly empty dining-room. The old, rambling, yellow stucco hotel is not centrally air-conditioned, the heat is oppressive, and flies are everywhere.

Our hosts have given us our itinerary to review. It is a tight schedule of meetings with women's groups and visits to hospitals, schools, orphanages, and museums—a typical agenda when visiting a country as guests of a sponsoring group. A tide of depression sweeps over me. Although I had taken for granted an agenda such as the one we face, I had assumed that we would then be free to wander on our own and would be taken to see other parts of Afghanistan. How was it that I hadn't taken it in when Miagol told us that the country was in the midst of a civil war?

My spirits revive the next day when Shakira and Zahera say that they had to leave us so quickly the previous night to return to their families because we had arrived on Eid-e-Qurban, a major Muslim holiday and, even in Communist Afghanistan, a national holiday. Women customarily prepare festive dinners for family gatherings, and Shakira was worried because her traditional husband expected her to be at home, instead of showing the sights to some American women. I laugh when she admits this, and tell her about the many times I had been at a demonstration or an international conference instead of home with my husband and children. Except that my husband and family were supportive of what I was doing.

Sweet-faced, eager, and outgoing, Shakira is in her early forties and looks very American—a bit plump, with a short haircut and Western-style clothes. She is an English-language professor at Kabul University. "Oh, my God!" she says breathlessly that first morning as we get to know each other. "You are the first native English speakers I have ever been with! I am scared to death!"

"Oh, my God!" turns out to be one of her favorite English expressions, a form of punctuation for her stories. "I do not just put the milk pitcher on the table and a glass beside his plate," she says, describing how she waits on her husband. "I must pour the milk into his glass. I cannot just put bread and butter on the table. I must butter his bread. He never tells me that something tastes good, but if he doesn't like it. Oh, my God! Kill me! I want to die."

It turns out that her husband, an airplane mechanic, is typical. At every meeting we go to we are told that with few exceptions Afghan men—even men in the Communist Party, even young men in the university—are traditionally opposed to women being politically active. Most of the women we meet began their political work in secret.

Shakira, her husband, and their four sons live in a two-bedroom apartment in an old building. One son is presently in Moscow at a university; two sons share a bedroom; and the youngest sleeps in the living room, which is also where the family eats. "My kitchen is so small that I bump against the wall as

I cook, and we have no shower or bathtub so we must all sponge bathe from a bucket of water," Shakira tells us. Every morning before she meets us, she hand washes everyone's clothes, irons, cleans, and prepares all the meals.

As a young girl, Shakira says, she felt strongly about the inequality of people and the condition of women. Her story is not an unusual one among educated, urban Afghans. She spent fifteen years as a member of the All-Afghan Women's Council, which had been illegal during the reign of Zahir Shah, without her husband knowing about her underground activities. But she was always afraid he would find out. When he did finally discover her secret political life, "there was much negative reflection," she says. She continued her "struggle," as she puts it, and now, she happily reports, "I don't even have any trouble with my husband or his family."

Zahera is more serious than Shakira. Perhaps for this reason, I feel more affinity with her. Tall, well built, and also always dressed in Western clothes, including pearl earrings and a simple brooch, Zahera unfailingly appears dignified, yet gentle. Some days her engaging six-year-old daughter, Leila, comes with her on our tours. Leila looks just like her mother, the same high cheekbones, long, thick, curly hair, and sweet, laughing eyes. She is very shy and generally hangs back from us. Most unusually, Zahera was married late, to a widower, a man she worked with politically. I gather that they have an exceptional, mutually respectful relationship and that Zahera has no difficulty with her political responsibilities.

Our host group, the All-Afghan Women's Council, was founded in the 1920s during the reign of King Amanullah. During its long history, the council has survived by accommodation, but the focus has always been on empowering women and rendering assistance where needed. While we are in Afghanistan, the council calls for a compromise settlement with the mujahidin so that reconstruction of the country can begin.

Our first meeting is with the council, at their bungalow provided by the government. At that point, I have no glimmering of how untypical the comfortable chairs, the flowers on side tables, and the coffee table set with tea and cookies are. All the women wear Western dress, mostly silk prints. On the streets in Kabul many women wear the burqa, although it is common to see women walking down the street together, one in a short skirt, another in a burqa with the top thrown back and the front left open, swinging back and forth, as she walks. Women appear to be free to wear what they choose. Nothing I see leads me to believe that women's clothes will become a battleground of deep symbolic and political importance when, two years later, the government is overthrown by the mujahidin.

Women from the council often visit refugee camps in Pakistan and Iran, where millions of Afghans fled during the war against the Soviets. "We go," one woman tells us, "to provide some education, even some work for the women, and to bolster their morale." Another breaks in, "The mullahs dominate the camps. Women are even more oppressed there than in traditional families here. When women in the camps go outside, they must be completely covered by the burqa, the girls get no schooling, and there is little opportunity for the women to earn a living."

On another day, we meet with a group supported by the council, called the Families of Martyrs, which was organized in 1985 to provide for widows and mothers who had lost husbands and children in the war. These women are more traditional than the political women of the council. They wear long dresses and shawls over their hair, or burqas with their faces uncovered.

Each woman's story is more horrifying than the one before. Fatima, young and very beautiful, her eyes a light seagreen, has a white scarf pushed back over her black hair. She had lived in a provincial village with her husband, a government army officer, and their six-year-old daughter. She was pregnant when the mujahidin attacked the village because it was in an area controlled by the government. Ten days after the fighting, she learned that her husband's body was at the bottom of a hill out-side the village. She sobs as she describes how birds had eaten away his eyes. She wanted to bring his remains back to the vil-lage but could not do it herself, so she asked her sister-in-law for help. The mujahidin were there, waiting, when the two women returned. They said she could have the body but they would take her sister-in-law. The young woman has not been seen since, and Fatima weeps as she considers the girl's fate.

Following another attack, Fatima and other village women were taken to a mujahidin camp, where they were forced to become sexual slaves. She escaped with her daughter and infant, and somehow made her way to a refugee camp in Pakistan where her brothers lived. But mujahidin were also menacing refugees in the camp, so she set out again with both children, crossing back into Afghanistan, and this time managed to get herself and her two small children to Kabul to live with her hus-band's family.

Fatima is almost hysterical by now, as she describes her father-in-law's demand that she marry her brother-in-law, even though he is already married. According to Islamic law as it is being interpreted by some in Afghanistan, men can have four wives; widows are not allowed to remarry except to the husband's brother, even if the brother is a baby. If they try to marry some-one else, they lose their children to the former husband's family.

The stories go on and on. One woman, with tears streaming down her face, describes watching her son and his friends at play from her small kitchen window when suddenly a group of armed men passed through the village and casually turned on the chil-dren and shot them. Others tell of having their children brought home with arms or legs blasted away by land mines.

But not all the stories we hear are of helplessness against war and weapons. We are introduced to a woman named Fer-oza, who is older than the others, a large, powerful-looking woman dressed in a long black dress with a black shawl over her head. I am struck by her look of force and dignity. When the mujahidin attacked villages, they often killed the men and abducted the women. We are told that Feroza organized a defense committee of two hundred women to defend the women of her village. She went to the government in Kabul for weapons, and when the next attack came, the women were ready, able to protect themselves. Her village has been spared ever since. Feroza says she is the commander of seven thousand armed women around the region. While the numbers she cites strain credulity, I am nonetheless filled with admiration for her.

The women we meet never speak of abuse by the Russians, nor do they mention the people's hatred of the Soviet troops or the Afghan Communist government. Of course, they all come from villages in the countryside that are controlled by the government and its Soviet allies, and their homes are under attack by the mujahidin. The mujahidin, for all the women we speak to, are the enemy, referred to as "counter revolutionaries." But there is little love for the Soviets either. Although there are few signs of it in Kabul, I have read about the terrible destruction wrought by Soviet troops during the war. The Soviets had sent in 120,000 combat troops, including thousands of elite Spetsnaz soldiers, their equivalent of the Green Berets. The invasion was led by tanks and armored personnel carriers, bristling with heavy machine guns and rockets, and with tactical air support.

As Afghans organized to resist the Soviets and the Afghan Communist government, three countries provided their main support: the United States, which used the mujahidin as Cold War proxies against the Russians; Saudi Arabia, which claimed that the mujahidin were holy warriors; and Pakistan, which sought an opening wedge for its own interests in Afghanistan. Thus the mujahidin were generously supplied with lethal modern weaponry. In 1983, Congressman Charlie Wilson, working with the CIA, provided them with US portable surface-to-air Stinger missiles, which destroyed Soviet air superiority. In response, the Soviets bombed villages and farms, poisoned wells, killed livestock, and tortured and murdered civilians. Over half the Afghan population fled their homes.

And now Gabi, Cynthia, and I are sitting with women who have been caught between these forces, and we are constantly brought to tears by their heartrending stories. Equally upsetting is the way they plead, "Tell our stories. Tell the American people. If they only know, they will stop arming the mujahidin." There is no way we can explain to these women that we are "outsiders" in the American power structure, that we have no influence on our government. The contrast between how blithely I have come on this trip and what these women expect of me becomes more oppressive as the appeals multiply everywhere we go.

Early each morning, to maintain my equanimity, I take a solitary walk in the hotel's overgrown, luxuriant garden. The old arthritic gardener who putters among the trees and flowers always greets me with a warm smile. As I wander down the paths, I look up at streaks of light, magnesium flares that flash across the sky to divert missiles from Arianna Airlines' scheduled flights. I fantasize that I am in an ancient Islamic garden. I name each flower and tree: There are orange poppies, old pink and white roses, spectacular sunflowers that open wider every morning and that I photograph each day. Purple wisteria and lavender rose of sharon bloom alongside lilac and multicolored anemones. Shasta daisies and petunias, red geraniums and brilliant zinnias grow entangled with each other. There are cedars and a eucalyptus tree.

When I leave the garden, we begin our daily crisscross of Kabul to our many meetings, always accompanied by a caravan of small automobiles that carry armed men for our protection. It seems a poor and weary city, not like the one described by Robert Byron in *The Road to Oxiana* where a boulevard designed by King Amanullah is said to be "One of the most beautiful avenues in the world—four miles long, lined with tall white-stemmed poplars. In front of the poplars run streams confined by grass margins. Behind them are shady foot-walks and a tangle of yellow and white roses." In 1990, the broad avenues are almost empty, although the narrow side streets teem with jostling people. Along these lanes open store fronts overflow with household merchandise and wagons are piled high with spices, fruits, and vegetables. There are lovely old tiled mosques and large Romanesque palaces, now used for museums and government offices. Farther out, on dusty unpaved streets, are clusters of houses built of mud-brick, and hundreds of large metal shipping containers, ubiquitous in developing countries, used for everything from workshops and makeshift factories to neighborhood markets. The encircling hills seem very close.

One day, our hosts accede to our complaints about being confined, and our caravan of cars drives up a perilous, stony road so we can get out and walk through a village among dwellings that from a distance had looked as though carved out of rock. The ruins of an ancient stone wall run up and over the higher hills. From the heights, sand-colored Kabul is dotted with the green of trees and parks, and the Kabul River sends out sparkles of light.

But we have little time for respite, as our rounds of visits and tours continues. We are taken to two government orphanages. Wars beget orphans. At the orphanage for babies, all dressed in blue pajamas, some of them are active and respond with delight to the candy we bring. Others are dull-eyed, too listless to respond. There are about five hundred babies in the institution, but adoptions are not allowed because family members might return for them after the war. As we find everywhere we go, most of the directors and staff are women, replacing tens of thousands of men killed or disabled in the war. The government seems to be doing its best to provide for the children while appeals for help to the international community go unanswered because the Communist government is under boycott by the West.

Another day we meet with Suraya Parlika, director of the Red Crescent, the equivalent of the Red Cross in Islamic countries. Her uncle, Abdul Wakil, is the foreign minister. I am especially interested when she mentions Peace Village—a community in Oberhausen, Germany, which I had visited three years earlier, where an extraordinary group of doctors and nurses treat and fit disabled children from war-torn areas with prosthetic limbs. As of 1990, Afghanistan, which leads the world in the number of unexploded land mines, has sent six hundred children to the Peace Village through the Red Crescent.

Two special days have been set aside for visiting our hosts' workplaces. We go first to the trade school for adult women that Zahera directs. The women are taught tailoring, weaving, and embroidery, along with literacy, nutrition, and family hygiene. A museum of tribal garments is on the top floor, and some of the younger women, as well as Zahera's daughter, Leila, put on a fashion show for us, dressed in the old, elaborately designed, richly-colored robes.

We also spend an afternoon at the university where Shakira teaches, roaming the lovely campus where students, dressed in jeans and T-shirts like students the world over, lounge under the shade of great old trees. The university, which opened for classes in 1932, began with many foreign instructors, but now has an all-Afghan faculty of six hundred, including some two hundred women. Women presently make up 60 percent of the students since many of the male students have died in the war. Education at all levels is free, with stipends for university students. Clearly, many Afghans do not have access to the university even with the stipends—the rural majority, especially. Still, no other Muslim country in the world does so much to encourage higher education.

As the holidays wind down, our hotel comes to life. We witness three lavish weddings with elaborate dinners, large bands, and dancing, fueled with alcoholic beverages. The young brides, dressed in Western-style gowns, as has been the fashion since the days of Amanullah, are so heavily painted with cosmetics they look like dolls. Family men, stout in dark business suits, stand together gossiping while the corseted women, dressed in glittering sequined and beaded dresses, move heavily around in their spike-heeled, dyed-to-match shoes. They are the only overweight people I ever encounter in Afghanistan. After dinner, the young people and men dance, boy with boy, girl with girl, man with man, while the women sit against the wall, watching and gossiping. These celebrants are some of the seventy-five thousand civil servants who, with the help of Soviet funds, maintain the government of President Mohammad Najibullah. The hovering shadow of the encircling mujahidin warriors lends a surreal cast to the lavish parties of this bureaucratic class.

Some of the more religiously moderate of the mujahidin are in negotiation with the Najibullah government and appear at the hotel one day. I stare at their bearded faces, their coarsely woven, layered robes, folded woolen caps or turbans of twisted patterned cloth. Miagol's comment to Gabi in Washington that members of the government are not the good guys to the average Afghan barely resonates in my consciousness. For me, Kabul is the whole of Afghanistan and the women who fear the mujahidin are now my friends.

When not on excursions, we often sit in the hotel lobby and talk to any other guests who speak English, including the few journalists covering events in the country. Deeda Tripathi, an Indian national with the BBC, had been denied entry during the occupation but has now been in Kabul for six months. Grinning with amusement, he tells us that he was denounced on Afghan television once a month on schedule during the occupation. He thinks the Najibullah government is far better than any of the other Soviet-backed ones and believes it should be recognized by the United States.

Leiz Doucet, with Canadian Public Broadcasting, lived in Kabul for a year and is now based in Islamabad, Pakistan. She is here visiting Afghan friends. Leiz says that the mullahs have increased their activity in the camps in Pakistan and that the intimidation of women has worsened as the mullahs' authority has expanded. The mullahs are building a power base, she says, in preparation for the struggle for control of the government as Afghan refugees flow back into the country following the Geneva Accord for mutual disengagement, negotiated between US Secretary of State James Baker and Soviet Foreign Minister Eduard Shevardnadze. The mullahs are waging a campaign of terror not only against women but also against Western relief agencies, whose educational and social programs threaten their concept of Islam. Several humanitarian groups have already left Pakistan because of death threats to their members.

I first hear the name Gulbuddin Hekmatyar from Leiz, who describes him as the most murderous zealot among all the mujahidin commanders. He is a favorite of Pakistan's military and received the largest percentage of the $3 billion that the United States sent during the Soviet war to arm the mujahidin. Leiz describes him as ambitious, wily, and anti-Western and says he has been accused of being a drug smuggler and counterfeiter. "He is the most intelligent of the mujahidin," she says, "but the most dangerous."

Zahera had known Hekmatyar in the 1960s when they were both at Kabul University. An engineering student, he had been a charismatic political firebrand. As Leiz describes him, Zahera listens quietly, then pulls Leila close to her and joins the conversation. "He was known on campus," she says, "for throwing acid at a woman's face because she was not covered." Zahera tenderly kisses Leila and adds softly, "I greatly fear him." I long to embrace the two of them but feel a barrier. Although I have grown to love Zahera, I feel it is somehow unseemly to intrude upon that most intimate connection between mother and child, especially when I do not share their circumstances. I can get out. I am the visitor from another world.

One of the most emotional visits for me is to the psychiatric wing of a general hospital. It brings to mind my beloved daughter, who spent years of her life in a psychiatric hospital. This

Afghan unit, a facility for long-term female patients, is in a compound separate from the main building, surrounded by low walls with perhaps a dozen two-room cottages. Cots are squeezed alongside each other, covering most of the floor space in each small room. A nurse accompanies us but does not speak. As we enter the grassy, tree-lined compound, a young woman patient with a badly scarred face rushes over and appoints herself our guide. She speaks English well and begins to wail that she is not "crazy"—and at first it seems she is not. Her husband, she laments, threw acid on her face because she was beautiful and he was jealous. The nurse nods confirmation. How did the woman learn to speak English so well? Had she been politically active? I want to learn her history, but I never do, since she becomes increasingly agitated as she takes us through the cottages and introduces us to the other patients, many with their mothers sitting beside them.

That scarred woman, the women suffering mental illness, the constant interviews with women whose stories fill me with dread, begin to unnerve me. I feel anxious and worried about all of them and the children. Yet at the same time, albeit with shame, I feel growing within me a pinching, cold fear for myself. Shakira and Zahera are clearly and increasingly worried about the approaching fighters. I begin to experience a submerged panic. Many nights I do not turn off my lamp for fear of waking in the dark, yet I also worry that my light might shine through the window and create a target.

After the hospital visit, I have one of my worst nightmares. There is a black-veiled, desperate woman; she is not me, but I know I am there and I, like her, have to escape. The surroundings are shrouded, gray. Suddenly, white-bearded mullahs loom up, black robes flowing. The veiled woman and I are running, running. An ancient stone fortress rises above us, deep mists swirl, the shrouded woman goes up, up, up circling steps—she might get away from the mullahs! My heart pounds. She is on a high battlement. But suddenly the mullahs are there! I plead, she pleads. The mullahs' arms wave, threatening. And then I plunge from the roof, falling down, down, screaming. I wake up, panting and sweating, staring around the room, trying to get my bearings.

"Why am I here? I want to get this trip over with!" I write in my journal. How mistaken I had been to believe that this would be a lark, an adventure in an interesting ancient Muslim country with a war somewhere off in the distance. And yet I already intuit that I am changing in a way I do not yet understand. It has to do with fear, a searing emotion I have never before truly understood. Of course, I have been afraid in my life, but it has never been anything like this endless, anxious terror of unknown danger lurking over the city. Fear is forging a bond between me and these women and this country.

The local TV carries daily news reports of our meetings. We are billed as American friends of Afghanistan. I feel like a fraud, since I know how meaningless this "friendship" is in terms of any help from my country to theirs. If anything, these broadcasts will only end up in CIA files.

Toward the end of our visit, one of Shakira's uncles invites us to his apartment for dinner, and we learn that he and some of her other relatives are highly placed in Communist circles. At the time of our visit, this uncle heads the Communist Party's Committee on Foreign Policy, but he had earlier been an ambassador to an Eastern European country. The huge apartment complex where he lives reminds me of the World War II–era housing project in Berkeley where I lived with my former husband and our infant twins when my husband was a graduate student. It gives me some insight into the level of the Afghan economy in 1990, as well as Kabul's critical housing situation, that this is the best his important position can provide. But Shakira thinks the apartment is wonderful and dreams of having one like it. She has brought her husband, who seems a rough, uneducated man, and her youngest son.

Shakira's uncle is warm and gracious, politically astute, and sophisticated. Like Miagol in Washington, he believes that the government party, the PDPA, had made a grievous error in calling upon the Soviets. Again Gabi challenges this position. The uncle seems bemused by her, but I am embarrassed at what I consider her classic American arrogance.

Shakira and her uncle are both members of the PDPA, which had been formally set up on New Year's Day 1965 while Afghanistan was still a monarchy. They give us a brief history of the party, which was unique among Communist parties loyal to the Soviet Union in that it quickly split into two distinct and murderously rival factions: Khalq (Masses) and Parcham (Banner). The split reflected cultural, ethnic, and class factors in Afghanistan, Shakira's uncle tells us. Both factions, however, recruited among the 5 percent of the country who were literate. Khalq was strongest among the rural educated, the military, and those who hated the royal family. It endorsed radical action to impose social change, but believed that women belonged in the home. Parcham drew its support from the urban educated class and included left-leaning members of the wealthiest, most powerful families; it functioned almost as a loyal opposition to the monarchy. Women were welcomed and important.

After the Communist coup in April 1978, the head of Khalq became president and Parcham leaders were soon purged—jailed or ordered into diplomatic exile. That was when Shakira's uncle, who had joined Parcham, was sent to Eastern Europe and Dr. Mohammad Najibullah—who would later become president—was sent to Tehran. Khalq's reign was Byzantine; terror became the norm and rival comrades were frequently assassinated. Shakira was arrested for a short time, along with other feminist members of Parcham such as Suraya Parlika, the head of Red Crescent, whom we had met earlier. Repeating Amanullah's mistake, the Khalq Communists enforced immediate social reforms, including bringing women into full civic participation, that were viewed as anti-Islamic by religious forces. Interparty violence continued amid growing resistance by the mass of the Afghan people. The Khalq chief, in desperation, called upon the Soviets for help and on Christmas Eve 1979, the Soviet army rolled in, bringing to power a more moderate Afghan Communist leader, Babrak Karmal of the Parcham faction.

Perhaps our most important meetings in Afghanistan are with two female government ministers. Neither woman has been a member of the PDPA, but both have been leaders of our hosts, the Women's Council. I am told that President Najibullah recruited these two impressive women and other nonparty officials after the Soviet withdrawal as part of his effort to build national reconciliation under a multiparty system. At that time he also abandoned the PDPA name for his party and chose a more nationalist one, Waban, meaning Homeland, although many Afghans still use the original name.

We meet first with Saleha Farugie Aetemadi, Minister of Social Affairs. She is probably in her mid-forties and is pleasant but formal; she sits behind her large desk throughout our interview, flanked by a male assistant and Zahera, who is an old friend. Her important ministry combines labor, economic planning, and social security. The scope of her work is enormous, encompassing everything from employment training programs to refugee relocation to agricultural development, including land mine clearance.

Before the Communist coup, Aetemadi had been president of the Women's Council for a decade, so she is sensitive to the special needs of women. I am surprised and impressed that she has heard about Women Strike for Peace, which I helped found, and I take the lead in answering her close and intelligent questions about the American women's movement. At the end of our interview, Aetemadi demands of us, "You must be the voice of the Afghan women! Bring our desire for peace to the American women." I feel chastened again for having come to Kabul for personal gratification. I answer her with gravity but with a

sinking inward feeling that I can never live up to her expecta-
tions. I wonder what will happen to this impressive woman if
the mujahidin win the war.

Minister of Education Massouma Asmity Wardak is quite
different. Warm and informal, she leads us to a room adjoining
her office where we sit at ease on a cushioned divan and armchairs and are served tea. Older than Aetemadi, she is tall, state-
ly, with a gently commanding quality. When a TV crew comes
in to film us, as they have done at most of our interviews, she
drapes a shawl over her head.

Wardak's family is middle class, her mother went to university, and she herself is fluent in English. She tells us that the
building we are in was built by Americans and that many Americans had taught in Afghanistan before the "revolution," the
Communist coup. She is proud of the fact that since the revolution—and despite the war—illiteracy among women has been
reduced, and that primary schools for girls have been started in
many villages. Ninety percent of the country's teachers are
women as well as 50 percent of its doctors and nurses. I am
impressed, but assume that all of this has been accomplished
only in the towns controlled by the Communist government; I
wonder what is happening in the rest of Afghanistan.

Our last interview of the trip, arranged by the Women's
Council, is with President Mohammad Najibullah himself. We
are driven to a government-military complex surrounded by
high walls. Inside there is no traffic, neither pedestrian nor
vehicular, just several tanks and soldiers.

President Najibullah welcomes us with a brilliant smile.
He is warm and charming, thanks us for our visit, and speaks
about the need for peace and his hope that the United States
will aid Afghanistan with American specialists. He goes on to
say that his is a coalition government, dedicated to reconciliation. He hopes that all Afghans will return to help reconstruct
their country. He smiles as he says he does not need to remind
us that women constitute one-half of society and it is essential

that they work side-by-side with men. Najibullah adds that Afghanistan is an Islamic country, that all law is based on Islamic law, the sharia, and that the mullahs must be part of national reconciliation. Gabi turns visibly white after that last sentence and she forever after holds Najibullah in contempt. My impression of the president that day is of a magnetic, charismatic man. He is handsome, with strong features, coal black hair, dark eyes, and full lips. He wears an open-necked shirt and a black blazer. Watching and listening to him, it is almost easy to forget that before he became president, he headed KHAD, the Communist regime's fearsome secret service. Despite my doubts, I find myself wishing with all my heart that he can succeed in negotiations with the mujahidin and bring peace to the country.

After this visit, we jump into our car, already packed with our luggage, and rush to the airline office to pick up our tickets. After pushing our way through a crowd to the counter, we discover that even though the council had booked our tickets months earlier, there are no seats for us. Since I have never shared my fears with Cynthia and Gabi, I have not realized that they are as full of dread and as anxious to get away as I am. But I know it then, as we stand there in that crowded room, terrified we won't be able to leave.

Shakira takes charge. Using her extensive circle of relatives, she calls a cousin who holds an important position with Arianna Airlines, and in a short time, tickets are produced. Next we rush off to the airport, which is as noisy and crowded as the ticket office, startlingly different from the empty cavern we found on our arrival. Other scheduled passengers are clamoring to get out of the country, and everyone is told there is no space. Again Shakira comes to the rescue. She finds a friend who works for Arianna and the two women literally push and haul us onto our plane. I crush Shakira in a goodbye hug, blow a kiss to Zahera, and almost weeping, settle into my seat.

Flying over a snowcapped mountain range on our way to

India, I feel guilty and grieved to be leaving our two friends
behind, and I cannot stop thinking about all those other brave
women who are working to ease the burden of war, to educate,
to support others while the deadly threat of the mujahidin
hangs over them.

During our short stay in India, I become ill and as the illness grows more severe, I decide to fly back to the States ahead
of Cynthia and Gabi. When I reach home, I am hospitalized
in intensive care, suspected of having cholera. My physician
brother insists upon having an infectious disease consultant,
who discovers that I have been infected by Giardia lamblia, a
protozoa that one gets by drinking contaminated water. I
recover quickly, yet in a visceral way I never completely recover from what I have experienced. It is not only that I am
haunted by what may happen to Shakera, Zahera, and Leila
and all the women I have met. I have also become obsessed
with Afghanistan itself, and angry about the role my country
has played in its tragedy.

Chapter 2
Against the Taliban, 1992–2000

I have been an activist nearly all my life. I remember when I was ten years old and held my mother's hand as we walked on a picket line in front of the White House, she carrying a sign demanding support for the democratically elected Republican government of Spain. My parents and their friends were always discussing politics, at times vehemently and often around us kids, so I understood even at that age that Mother and I were protesting Franco's fascist insurgency, which was backed by the governments of Italy and Germany. Other Western governments, including the United States, did not support the Republicans, and the defeat of the Spanish government had deep repercussions. It foreshadowed World War II, when the world would have to confront the threat of fascism on a much larger scale. That history of the Spanish Civil War and the world's response to it would resonate in my experience of Afghanistan.

Both my parents had grown up in orthodox Jewish families—my mother in old Russia, my father in Brooklyn. They met in Manhattan in the socialist, secular milieu of the 1920s and after they married, moved to Washington, D.C. I was born there in 1925, in a city that was then a southern, segregated small town. I remember going with my father to see World War I Bonus Marchers—an army of unemployed veterans encamped on the nearby Anacostia hills.

Coming of age in times different from my parents', I went further afield politically than either of them, joining a Marxist student group at Antioch College, enduring hard times during the McCarthy era, and then turning to the New Left and the civil rights and anti-Vietnam War movements of the 1960s. As second-wave feminism gained ground, I became involved, and my worldview now encompasses gender as well as class and race. But I remain my mother's daughter; I have been demonstrating or organizing ever since those days beside her in front of the White House gates. I think she would not have been surprised by the paths I took and the places to which I journeyed. Nor would she be surprised by my growing commitment to Afghanistan.

By 1992, the mujahidin are close to overcoming the Kabul government, and I watch the news with trepidation. When Miagol, the Afghan Chargé d'Affaires in Washington, first told me about the mujahidin, I had conceived of them as one group. In fact, there are seven major organizations, led by rival conservative Muslims of varying degrees of religiosity, all of whom are politically ambitious men who head political parties that are generally ethnically based. They include Gulbuddin Hekmatyar, the man so feared by Zahera for his fanatic approach to Islam and his use of brutal violence to support his cause. In 1973, he was jailed for ordering the murder of a Maoist student. Although his party, Hezb-e-Islami (Islamic Party), continues to receive most of the millions that the CIA is funneling to the mujahidin through Pakistan's secret service, the Inter-Services Intelligence (ISI), he is rabidly anti-American. His most hated rival is the more moderate Ahmad Shah Massoud, defense minister of Burhanuddin Rabbani's party, Jamiat-e-Islami (Islamic Society), which is largely made up of ethnic Tajiks. The bitterly contentious relationship between Hekmatyar and Massoud began when both studied under Rabbani, then a Kabul University theology professor who had formed Afghanistan's first Islamist party.

Hekmatyar, an engineering student, and Massoud, a student of architecture, both joined Rabbani's demonstrations against the dissolution of the monarchy and the formation of the secular republic in 1973. When their nascent movement was quickly crushed, both young men, along with some five thousand other young Islamists, followed Rabbani into exile in Pakistan, where they were welcomed by President Zulfikar Ali Bhutto and given military training. In 1975, the Afghans were enlisted to join Pakistani incursions into their homeland. Massoud's lifelong mistrust of Pakistan began at that time, and in 1978, he returned to Afghanistan to develop an indigenous movement among the Tajiks in the Panjshir Valley north of Kabul. While Massoud remained loyal to Rabbani, Hekmatyar broke with his former professor to form a more radical Islamist party. Now, in 1992, the two rivals, each with his own troops, are at the outskirts of Kabul and are vying to be the first to enter the city.

In the United States there is very little information about any of this; Afghanistan is no longer newsworthy. Belatedly, I realize that I do not even know Shakira and Zahera's last names, or if they even have last names, or any way in which I can communicate with them. I search the media endlessly for information.

Unlike the US government, the United Nations and its Secretary-General, Boutros Boutros-Ghali, consider the fate of post-Soviet Afghanistan a matter of great concern. With some six million refugees (the highest number of any country in the world), more than two million dead, another two million disabled, an estimated ten million mines in the countryside, and the chaos that will inevitably result from the fall of Najibullah, Afghanistan could become a major disaster zone. In the spring of 1992, the UN sends a mission to Kabul with the aim of ensuring a peaceful and stable transfer of power to an interim authority that will prepare for elections.

Negotiations toward that goal take place in Peshawar, Pakistan, with national and international representatives, and envoys from the seven mujahidin groups. The final agreement, the Peshawar Accords, is for a fifty-one-person transitional government to take power for two months until a "Loya Jirga"—the traditional assembly of Afghan leaders that elects leaders, enact laws, or confronts a crisis—can be convened to prepare for elections. Najibullah has been persuaded to resign with the promise that he and his brother will be evacuated to India, where their families await them. He asks that one thousand international peacekeeping troops be stationed in Kabul, to ensure the orderly transfer of power, but Pakistan vehemently opposes the request—and since the United States supports Pakistan, the proposal is doomed. The entire negotiation process is muddied by rival mujahidin ambitions and the power of Pakistan to make demands. M. Hassan Kakar, an Afghan historian, has said of the accords, "It was not just Najib who was being held hostage. It was Afghanistan as well, although this time the kidnapper was neither Russia nor Great Britain, as in the Great Game. It was Pakistan."

With the accords signed, Najibullah and his party are being escorted to the airport when their convoy is stopped by PDPA General Abdul Rashid Dostum, whose Uzbek party is based in the northern city of Mazar-i-Sherif. Najibullah is returned to Kabul, where he and his brother are given refuge in a UN compound. It is said that Najibullah spends his days translating a history of British-era Afghanistan and the Great Game.

In his last days in government, Najibullah had told reporters from the *International Herald Tribune*, "If fundamentalism comes to Afghanistan, war will continue for many years. Afghanistan will turn into a center of world smuggling for narcotic drugs. Afghanistan will be turned into a center for terrorism."

Kabul falls to the mujahidin on April 25, 1992. Many government troops go over to Massoud, who is the first leader to enter the city, riding on a tank strewn with flowers. According to news accounts, hundreds of Massoud's mujahidin fire their assault rifles into the air in celebration, but by the next day they have lowered their rifles and are aiming them at other troops as fighting breaks out with other mujahidin groups who have followed him into the city. It is said, "The first Afghan war is over. The second has begun." As I sit in Washington reading the brief news reports, I can hardly bear to imagine Zahera's fear, or how the council women will survive. April 25 is my birthday, and as I move through the day, so freely, so privileged, I am overwhelmed once again by the fact that we Americans are so removed from the calamitous results of our country's foreign intrusions.

According to the Peshawar Accords, each of the seven mujahidin commanders is to serve, on a rotating basis, as president of the interim government until elections can be held. I am appalled to read that when the two women ministers whom we had interviewed, Saleha Farugie Aetemadi and Massouma Asmity Wardak, join their male colleagues from the outgoing government to pay respects to the new mujahidin president, Sibghatullan Mujaddedi (Sibghatullah) Mujaddedi, his aides turn them back because their long black dresses fail to conceal their ankles.

Rabbani's turn is next and when it is over, he refuses to relinquish the position. Hekmatyar has already rejected the whole process and retreated to his base in the surrounding hills to begin relentlessly pounding the city with hundreds of rockets. Kabul, which survived a ten-year war against a foreign occupation, is being destroyed by its own people. I begin to get information from an Afghan Listserv on the Internet and learn that militia groups make alliances one day and become enemies the next. Rape and civilian executions are becoming the norm. Electric grids are failing throughout towns, food supplies are shrinking, and disease is spreading. In 1994, some ten thousand civilians die violently. Anarchy and chaos spread from Kabul throughout Afghanistan. The people are desperate.

Then, awful news—the Taliban has entered Afghanistan from Pakistan. Talib militias trained for jihad in Pakistani madrassas—Islamic religious schools—are joined by Arab troops, with military aid from Pakistan, and are being welcomed by the Pashtun populace of the southern city of Kandahar. The Taliban promises the desperate people that they will operate under sharia law to restore civil order from the chaos created by the mujahidin civil war.

As I watch all this take place from afar, I also begin to educate myself about the vast sums and advanced weapons that our government has invested over the years in the mujahidin. I am stunned to learn just how provocative my country's role has been in this tragic war. Early in the summer of 1979, several months before the Soviet invasion, President Jimmy Carter had issued a directive to the CIA to provide covert aid to the Afghan rebels who were fighting the Communist government. It was a move that national security advisor Zbigniew Brzezinski hoped would "trap" the Russians, in his words, and "give the USSR its Vietnam."

During the 1980s, students were recruited and trained for jihad in Afghanistan through a string of new madrassas established by Saudi Arabia in Pakistan to proselytize Wahhabism, the Saudi fundamentalist branch of Sunni Islam. Many of these madrassas were also boarding schools for refugee Afghan boys and indigent Pakistanis. It was not long before there were more than eight hundred official schools along the Afghan-Pakistani border. According to Ahmed Rashid, author of the bestselling book *Taliban*, "Tens of thousands [of] foreign Muslim radicals came to study in the new madrassas [and] between 1982 and 1992, some 35,000 Muslim radicals from 43 Islamic countries [including] Filipino Moros, Uzbeks from Soviet Central Asia, Arabs from Algeria, Uighurs from Xinjiang in China, Egypt, Saudi Arabia and Kuwait ... would pass their baptism under fire with the Afghan mujahidin." The recruitment and funding was not limited to Saudi Arabia, but included the Muslim Brotherhood, the radical Islamist group that was founded in Egypt and has repeatedly been banned there, and the CIA, under William

Casey, all organized by the ISI, and aided by Hekmatyar's Heizb-e-Islami. The wealthy Saudi, Osama bin Laden, also helped fund the mujahidin during the Soviet war, and in 1989 set up Al Qaeda to develop broad-based alliances with Arab militants.

By 1994, Pashtun mujahidin, grouped around an uneducated village mullah, Muhammed Omar, have joined forces with fundamentalist students and have taken control of Kandahar. And from there they orchestrate a fundamentalist movement to cleanse Afghanistan of Western influence and make it the purest Islamic state in the world in accordance with their own views of Islam and sharia law.

The Taliban's first decrees in Kandahar are aimed at the status of women: they may not work outside the home; they must wear the burqa—a heavy garment covering the head and body with only a small gauze inset to see through—in public; schools for girls and women must shut down, along with nearly all public places where women gather, such as female bathhouses; women may not be seen by non-relative males or be treated by male doctors. The edicts of repression multiply. Women who display a single finger outside the burqa can have it chopped off. A woman meeting with a man who is not a relative can be stoned to death.

Prayer becomes obligatory for men, who are no longer allowed to shave their beards. All forms of entertainment, including the national pastime of kite-flying, are prohibited; musical instruments, singing, television, chess, all celebrations (such as wedding receptions), are forbidden. Smoking and alcohol, forbidden. Normal government structure, eliminated. All authority stems from Taliban commissions and Islamic tribunals. Punishment is severe, archaic, and immediate.

I follow what little news there is of the Taliban militias, reinforced by thousands of Arab and Pakistan contingents, as they battle their way across the country. In 1996, they finally enter Kabul, while the warring rival mujahidin fade into the populace, join the Taliban, or go into exile in neighboring countries. Only Massoud and his Tajik forces are determined to resist the Taliban; he withdraws from Kabul and moves north to his home base in the Panjshir Valley.

The Taliban's first act on capturing Kabul is to drag Najibullah and his brother from the UN compound where they have stayed for the past four years. Up to this time, the warring factions have respected the diplomatic immunity of the UN, so this is a deliberate act of defiance against the world organization. Najibullah and his brother are beaten senseless, then taken to the presidential palace, where both men are tortured and Najibullah is castrated and dragged behind a jeep. My stomach turns when I see photos in the media of their bloated bodies hanging from a traffic control post in the city.

I am beginning to understand another aspect of my obsession with Afghanistan. Since my visit there, I have felt uneasily apart from my own culture. People in the United States just do not seem to understand the significance of the drama playing out in that distant part of the world, which I see as a terminal struggle between religiously based patriarchal authority and secular support for gender and ethnic equality. Almost vertiginously, I feel the political landscape I have known all my life fading and a new, still shadowy, terrain rising up around us. It seems to me that, in innocent ignorance, we are moving blindly through a global interregnum.

During most of my lifetime, two powerful countries, representing two opposing systems, have shared the world stage—the Communist USSR, and the capitalist United States. Their fierce eighty-two-year competition has been the overweening political discourse. That confrontation ended with the collapse of the Soviet system, and the apparent triumph of the United States. But, unseen and ignored by most of the world, a new force is coalescing in the back alleys of history, and I believe its genesis is in Afghanistan. I have come to see events there as an omen; Afghanistan as our modern Cassandra.

I am desperate to do something to help prevent the Taliban from taking over the entire country. As the Talibs have battled their way across Afghanistan, the US media has begun to report on their brutality against women and their degradation of Afghan society, yet no one seems to care that under Taliban decrees, every woman is literally denied the right to lift her bare face to the sky. Her condition is lower than that of a beast of burden, which can at least breathe fresh air. Even though many people I speak to are touched by the fact that girls are forbidden to study and women to work, the response is typically a what-can-I-do-about-it shrug.

I have found only one American activist organization whose work against the Taliban I agree with: the Feminist Majority Foundation. There is also an Afghan women's group, RAWA (Revolutionary Association of the Women of Afghanistan), based in Pakistan, that has captured the imagination of many Americans with its dramatic exposure of the plight of Afghan women, but I am most impressed by Ellie Smeal, the Feminist Majority's president, and her analysis of the global significance of the Taliban's extremist religious misogyny: "We have been saying for years that a country where so many people have no rights will create international instability," she says. "People just thought, 'Oh, there they go about the women again.' People need to realize that women are important, not just in their own right, but that we're the canaries in the coal mine. How women are treated is a good indication of which way society is going." Ellie's position is that the international community's passive acceptance of the Taliban's brutalities is a threat to all free civil societies.

The Feminist Majority has launched a "Campaign to Stop Gender Apartheid," with the goal of putting the condition of women in Afghanistan on a par with the oppression of blacks in South Africa, an injustice that inspired international opposition. Its first priority is to stop the United States from recognizing the Taliban as the legitimate government of Afghanistan.

While only Pakistan, Saudi Arabia, and the United Arab Emirates have recognized the Taliban government, the United States is not unfriendly. The Clinton administration effectively supports the Taliban through its allies Pakistan and Saudi Arabia. In addition, Unocal, an American energy corporation, is negotiating intensely for a pipeline from Turkmenistan, newly independent of the Soviet Union, through Afghanistan to Pakistan and the shipping lanes of the Indian Ocean. The pipeline would bring the Taliban royalties of some one hundred million dollars a year. The Clinton administration supports the project, and apparently believes that a stable government, no matter what its politics, offers the best prospects for the pipeline being built and operating without threat. The Feminist Majority, aided by its board member Mavis Leno, wife of late-night TV host Jay Leno, is fighting back with ads, public meetings, and petitions. Bombarded by the political and wealthy feminist women in Hollywood, Hillary Rodham Clinton and Secretary of State Madeline Albright are also beginning to take a public stand against the Taliban.

In the summer of 1999, I hold a fundraiser for the Feminist Majority on Martha's Vineyard. Hawa Ghaus, a young Afghan staffer at the foundation, in a brilliant presentation, compares the Taliban to the Cambodian Khmer Rouge. Both groups, she points out, were and are fanatically committed to their visions of a former golden age in their respective countries, and remorseless in their destruction of whatever has stood in their way. While the Khmer Rouge's vision of a rural communal utopia required the destruction of Cambodia's educated population and its urban infrastructure, the Taliban's vision of an international Islamic caliphate requires the total subjection of women, because emancipated women typify modernity, equality, and, frequently, secularism.

I admire the Feminist Majority for their campaigns, but I want to work directly with women from Afghanistan. I seek out the large Afghan community in northern Virginia, where most of the refugees are from the first exodus, those who fled the Russians, and many of them, both women and men, are working successfully in business and the professions. A number of the women are engaged in aid projects, but they are studiously nonpolitical. The exception is Nasrine Gross, whom I meet in the fall of 2000 at her annual fund-raiser for women and children in Afghanistan.

Nasrine tells me that she had avoided politics most of her adult life until the Taliban took power. She became increasingly unhappy about what was happening to her country, but did not know what to do until she heard about a conference that would be held in the summer of 2000, in Dushanbe, Tajikistan. She was determined to go, and it changed her life. The gathering was the culmination of years of organizing inside Afghanistan, in refugee camps, and in European countries by Shoukria Haidar, a French Afghan physical education teacher in a private girls' school outside Paris. Shoukria, a whirlwind of a woman and a magnetic speaker, founded NEGAR—Support of Women of Afghanistan (in Dari, NEGAR's meaning is closest to "good companion") to educate the public about the situation of Afghan women under the Taliban militias and "to unveil the role played by Pakistan."

Beginning in 1997, NEGAR began to finance schools for girls in the north, starting with ten and quickly expanding to twenty-six. The schools were in regions not controlled by the Taliban militias, but under constant attack from them, and thus forced to abandon support for girls' education. School buildings in these areas had deteriorated or ceased to exist; courses took place in tents or village mosques without desks, chairs or school supplies; and teachers—98 percent of them women—were paid irregularly and inadequately. NEGAR began by paying teachers' salaries.

By 2000, NEGAR's primary goal was to work for a political solution to end the war and reestablish the rights of women in Afghanistan. Shoukria decided to organize a conference that would bring together women from Afghanistan as well as the diaspora, to write a Declaration of the Essential Rights of Afghan Women, and to begin an international campaign. Despite the dangers and difficulties of moving clandestinely through Taliban-occupied country and mullah-dominated refugee camps, some two hundred to three hundred Afghan women arrived in Dushanbe on June 28, 2000. They far outnumbered the women, like Nasrine, from the Afghan diaspora and the few Europeans. The declaration produced at the conference is a powerful statement, affirming that "the fundamental right of Afghan women, as for all human beings, is life with dignity." (The full text of the declaration appears at the end of this book.)

Nasrine was called upon to read the final document at the closing session. "I was trembling. It was hot and muggy but I was shivering—with apprehension and hope," she later wrote. "As I finished the last word, I was afraid to look up and see the reaction. But then I saw a colleague with tears in her eyes standing up and cheering and dancing. So powerful was this message of inalienable rights and so great the sense of promise that even those who did not understand Dari cried and clapped and hugged."

After returning to the United States from the Dushanbe conference, Nasrine abruptly closed her business and became a full-time activist as the US representative of NEGAR. Nasrine was born in Kabul in 1945 to a prominent Tajik/Pashtun family. Her mother, Roqia Habibi, had participated in the women's emancipation movement during the 1950s, and two of her uncles were among the seven men who drafted Afghanistan's progressive 1964 constitution. Roqia was a member of the 1965 Loya Jirga that endorsed the new constitution, and she was one of four women elected to parliament the following year.

Nasrine's father, Abou Bakre, was a distinguished scholar. A student of physics at France's University of Montpelier in the late 1930s, he was stranded there by World War II, and returned to Kabul as Afghanistan's first European Ph.D. He founded Kabul University's physics department and eventually became university president. Like so many other democrats in the tumultuous 1960s, Dr. Abou Bakre spent time in prison. When he was unable to continue his academic career, he became a businessman and contractor.

Nasrine had come to the United States in 1971, not as an exile but with her American husband, Max Gross, a Korean War veteran from Iowa, whom she had met when both were students at the American University in Beirut. He converted to Islam in order to marry her, since Muslim women are allowed to marry only Muslims, although Muslim men may marry another monotheist such as a Jew or a Christian. They moved to Washington, D.C., where Nasrine developed a computer programming business and raised a son. She researched and wrote two books in Dari. The first was a volume of interviews with former students and their families from the pathbreaking Malalay High School, Afghanistan's first secondary school for girls, which both Nasrine and her mother had attended. The other book was about traditional conflict resolution practiced in Afghanistan.

I am drawn to Nasrine and NEGAR as soon as I meet her; I want to work directly with Afghan women and I agree with NEGAR's program, which is simply about the equality of women. I also agree with NEGAR's political goal of peace and the restoration of a constitutional government in Afghanistan, and like the fact that it is not attached to any political party. Shoukria's French group has developed a petition to the UN, calling for a meeting of Afghanistan's immediate neighbors, Pakistan, Iran, China, and Russia, as well as the United States, to negotiate a constitutional government that will recognize women's rights. They seek a million signatures, worldwide, to be presented by a group of prominent international personalities backed by a mass gathering.

During the winter of 2000/2001, a group of us, led by Nasrine, struggle to translate the French petition into English, using
language that will be politically acceptable to a broad spectrum
of Americans, who are not as knowledgeable as the French
about the situation in Afghanistan, and in particular, about the
role of Pakistan in providing support and a base for the Taliban
and Al Qaeda. In addition to endorsing the declaration, signers
are asked to lobby their political leaders on three points: to prevent our government from recognizing the Taliban, to pressure
Pakistan to end its intervention in Afghanistan, and to work
with the UN to begin a peace process in Afghanistan.

We want signatures from national and local political leaders, well-known personalities in feminist, civil rights, and human
rights communities, as well as average Americans whom we
reach out to at meetings and on the streets. Nasrine is tireless,
speaking everywhere, picking up allies and always distributing
copies of the petition. She meets frequently with State Department officers for Afghanistan and for women's affairs; she works
the halls of Congress, successfully getting signatures from
Republicans and Democrats alike. In New York, I introduce her
to the Women's Environment and Development Organization
(WEDO), founded by Bella Abzug, and to Judy Lerner, a long-
time friend from Women Strike for Peace, who works with
peace-related groups at the UN. Judy introduces Nasrine around
the UN, and the response to her talks is so enthusiastic that
Nasrine calls Shoukria and tells her to come to New York.

One morning in February 2001, our group learns that a rov-
ing ambassador of the Taliban, Sayed Rahmatullah Hashemi,
has arrived in the United States to speak to important foreign
policy groups. Under the UN sanctions, high-level Taliban officials are barred from traveling abroad, but the Taliban foreign
ministry has been able to arrange meetings at the State Department and to book several speaking engagements for him. His
only public appearance in Washington will be at the Atlantic
Council, a club for foreign policy mavens and diplomats. Admis-

sion is by invitation only, but I am able to get one, representing the Institute for Women's Policy Research, where I am a long-time board member.

On the day of the talk, dressed professionally and carrying a briefcase, I walk past NEGAR's demonstration outside the Atlantic Council's Connecticut Avenue building and into the walnut-paneled boardroom of the club. Camera crews are set up in the back, and men—mostly white and mostly white haired—sit in the armchairs that circle the podium. Rahmatullah, elegantly attired in a silk version of traditional Afghan dress, gets up to speak. He insists that the West is misinformed about the Taliban's programs and methods, which, he says, are only part of an effort to restore peace and order. When he finishes speaking, the audience begins to ask questions, but before he can answer, I stand up, pull a burqa from my briefcase, and fling it over my head. Then I loudly confront him with statements about the true nature of the Taliban. The cameras turn on me, while the men nearby pull away in horror. The meeting ends in a state of confusion as I walk out. That kind of dramatic confrontation has never come easily to me, but I know how important the media attention is for our cause and, years later, even enjoy a brief moment of fame as friends around the world see that confrontation in Michael Moore's documentary *Fahrenheit 9/11*.

But most of my work with NEGAR is not so dramatic. During the many hours I spend working with Nasrine, I develop enormous respect for her. However, I am growing uneasy about differences between my world outlook and that of the Afghan women. Nasrine and Shoukria greatly admire and respect the mujahidin commander, Ahmad Shah Massoud, who played a major role in defeating the Soviets and is now battling the Taliban.

During my 1990 trip to Kabul, my sympathies were with the women who considered the mujahidin counterrevolutionaries. At the same time, I understood that the people I was meeting were primarily echoing the Communist position, and that both the Soviet troops and the mujahidin had committed atrocities. Nevertheless, the mujahidin's beliefs are inimical to my own tenets. It feels contradictory to me that my new Afghan comrades, liberal and feminist, view the mujahidin as heroes because they fought the Russians. They appear to be willing to ignore the fact that the mujahidin are religious fundamentalists and that their position on civil rights and the equality of women is in opposition to our own. Now that mujahidin are allied with Massoud and fighting the Pakistan-Taliban alliance, support for them among my Afghan friends continues to grow even stronger. I do not know or understand the traditional loyalties and conflicts of Afghanistan that certainly play a role in Nasrine and Shoukria's thinking, and I do not want to be involved in even the slightest way with their internal politics and parties. I share my unease with old friends and, finally, have an intense debate with myself: Can I continue working with Nasrine and Shoukria and NEGAR?

I decide that my overriding issue is the Taliban's imminent threat to take over the whole of Afghanistan and impose its brutal interpretation of sharia law upon the people. NEGAR, a dynamic organization of women with an important petition campaign seems the best group to work with. I'm in.

I now want to learn more about this man Massoud, the military leader of the Northern Alliance, whom all my friends respect so much, and who is considered a brilliant strategist and a charismatic leader. His mythic reputation stems from the fact that he is said to have fought off seven major Soviet offensives in the Panjshir Valley. Russian generals called him unbeatable, a master of guerrilla warfare. His forces were the first to enter Kabul when the Najibullah government was overthrown. He barely survived the ensuing civil war and the Taliban conquests, and now, with his back to the wall, he continues to fight as commander of the Northern Alliance against the Pakistan-supported Taliban militias.

Massoud's appearance adds to his charisma. He has the

looks of a poet, with his thin, hawklike face; dark, brooding eyes, which even in photographs seem to smolder; and thick black hair topped by his traditional pakol cap. Born in 1953 to a Tajik family from the Panjshir Valley, Massoud was educated at the French lycée in Kabul. He reads French literature and is a lover of poetry. During interludes in the fighting, he has built a home for his family in the Valley, where he keeps a library of some three thousand volumes. A religious Muslim, he was a fundamentalist in his youth and is the military leader of the Islamist party led by Rabbani, although, I am told, he became disillusioned with his early mentor after the civil war debacle.

By the time I meet the women of NEGAR, Massoud has brought together opponents of the Taliban from every major Afghan ethnic group to transform the largely Tajik Northern Alliance into a United Front of mujahidin leaders, each with his own militias but with an agreement that has essentially made Massoud commander-in-chief. The most important and well known of the allied leaders include the Uzbek General Abdul Rashid Dostum, based in Mazar-i-Sharif; Ismail Khan, the governor of Herat; Karim Khalili, the Hazara Shiite leader; and Haji Qador, the Pashtun warlord-politician.

Massoud is receiving limited support from the bordering countries of Russia, Uzbekistan, and Tajikistan, all of which fear Taliban inroads among their own Muslim citizens. Shiite Iran, concerned about the Taliban Sunnis, also provides some aid. Even the CIA is belatedly giving Massoud direct funds. However, the total of this aid is insignificant compared with the war planes and heavy armaments that Pakistan is supplying to the Taliban along with thousands of young Pakistani fighters. Plus the Taliban have bin Laden's Arab jihad warriors.

One afternoon, a small group of us meet at Nasrine's home to hear a report from a Northern Alliance lobbyist just returned from Afghanistan. Otilie English is something of a surprise, a tall, blond, strapping North American who looks, in her khakis and boots, as though she has just returned from safari. Her brother, Phil English, is a Republican congressman from Pennsylvania. During the 1980s, she became a devoted supporter of the mujahidin fighting against the Soviets and a lobbyist for the anti-communist Committee for a Free Afghanistan. Obviously, her politics are far to the right of mine, but I am getting used to working in a "united front" against a common enemy, the Taliban.

As we gather around a coffee table, Otilie tears a leaf from her notebook and draws a sketchy map of Afghanistan to show us the area governed by Massoud's forces—a large territory, although not nearly as vast as the part-desert areas in the south populated by Pashtun clans that support the Taliban. What the Northern Alliance area lacks in size, she tells us, it makes up for in population density. Otilie points to the areas where she has recently trekked with Alliance forces. They nearly surround Kabul. If Otilie's information is accurate, it means that the situation is more complicated than we have understood. While Massoud and the Front may not have enough funds and weapons to go into full-scale battle against the military might of the Taliban, Al Qaeda, and Pakistan, they control a large area with great strategic value.

"Oh, how I long to go back," Nasrine cries, as she listens to Otilie's description of moving through the countryside.

"O.K., let's go," I say, surprising myself. Knowing she cannot afford it, I add, "I'll take care of it."

Once I have said it aloud, I know that going back is what I most want to do. And so, once again, I begin preparations to go to Afghanistan, this time starting with intense planning sessions. We will put together an American women's investigatory trip to the part of the country that has not been overrun by the Taliban. The Pakistan lobby has cast Massoud and the Northern Alliance as America's enemy, and they are generally seen here in the United States in the worst possible light. Our plan is to review, on the ground, the condition of women living in the area controlled by the Northern Alliance and then report back to women's groups, Congress, and the media.

Nasrine has to contact the Northern Alliance to get their agreement for us to travel through their region. She also arranges our complicated travel details, which include getting visas from the Afghan embassy in Munich and from Tajikistan, through which we will travel. Most travelers to Afghanistan get their visas from the Taliban and Pakistan, which, of course, we cannot do.

We hope to take with us at least one journalist with good media connections, a photographer, and several independent women who will join us in posttrip public speaking and lobbying. However, it is hard to garner much interest in Afghanistan. The trip is seen as problematic, expensive, and dangerous by the women we contact. I go over, again and again, with Nasrine, the probability of danger and the detailed costs. We are convinced that our on-site fact-finding and analysis will be effective with American feminists, will find outlets in the press, and will catch the attention of some political figures. In any case, the determining factor is that we want to go, and I can provide the means while Nasrine can provide the contacts.

Nasrine is worried that the Pakistan lobby in Washington, as well as our own government, may block our trip, so we keep a low profile and decide not to recruit women with organizational affiliations. A California filmmaker, Cindy Spies, who is producing a documentary on Mary MacMakin, an American who has lived in Afghanistan off and on for twenty-four years, agrees to send a camerawoman who will work with us and interview Mary. There is a limited time frame for our trip because of weather. Fog and heavy snow make helicopter travel perilous in the winter, and the intense heat and sandstorms of summer are also bad. The milder weather of early fall is best for travel—but also for battle. Since we have little choice, we make the final decision to go in late August of 2001, even though we have been unable to pull together the delegation we would have wanted. After some anxious weeks securing visas, getting shots, buying sleeping bags and hiking boots, and assuring my family and friends that I'll be safe, and back in less than two weeks, we head off. This time I know so much more about the country than I did eleven years ago. This time I do not go for the joy of an interesting trip before I grow old. I *am* old. I want to see and do something important with the rest of my life. For me, the Taliban has come to represent everything I have always fought against. With disbelief, I see the fundamentalist groups of all religions growing in numbers and strength in this new century. I continue to fear that the radical Muslim fundamentalists have the potential to become the same kind of threat to civil societies that the Nazis were fifty years earlier. I keep coming back to the parallels between the 1936 invasion of Spain by the Fascists under General Franco and the 1994 invasion of Afghanistan by the Taliban under Mullah Omar. Franco's invasion was heavily armed and supported by neighboring Germany and Italy. The Afghan Taliban invasion is abetted by neighboring Pakistan, with support from Saudi Arabia. In the 1930s, the democratic world turned its back on Spain. Now, the United States is withholding support from the Northern Alliance in favor of the "stable" military government of the Taliban. Fifty years earlier, Franco's fascist forces prevailed, and the war in Spain served as a prelude to the Nazi sweep through Europe, sparking a world war. Would the same thing happen now, I worried, with the Taliban and their supporters ruling much of the Middle East? Would our decision not to become involved prove as misguidedly wrong in Afghanistan as it had been in Spain?

Chapter 3
Journey to the Land
of the Mujahidin, 2001

Nasrine and I are flying via Germany, Turkey, and Tajikistan. We are joined by Sara, the twenty-seven-year-old Swiss student and videographer hired to film Mary MacMakin. Our flight arrives in Munich at 1:30 a.m., with a nine-hour wait before the plane to Dushanbe takes off. Our bags are unloaded for transfer to the Tajik plane, with the biggest belonging to Nasrine. They are filled with schoolbooks, many of them heavy medical texts. She has also packed notebooks, posters, maps, and globes, as well as medicines, toiletries, clothes, seed packets, and gifts. Sara has her heavy camera and equipment. I have the least, but my load is still bulky, with a bedroll, heavy walking boots, my Peruvian wool serape, and a number of gift-wrapped scarves. Plagued by the memory of how sick I had been after my last trip, I have also brought along four quart-size bottles of spring water and a small water-purification kit.

While most of the Afghan refugees are in Pakistani and Iranian camps, Tajikistan holds a sizable portion of the Afghan diaspora. Nasrine's plans for my one-week trip include only one day in Dushanbe, but it will be packed full: we will try to meet with the Afghan Women's Association, the Refugee Association, the Peace Institute, and a women's sewing workshop.

When we arrive in Afghanistan, we will stay one day at a

guesthouse the Northern Alliance maintains in the town of Khoja Bahauddin, where we will meet with the local women's association, and visit a camp for internally displaced refugees. Then on to the ancient town of Faizabad for two days, where Nasrine lists visits to a school, a university, a television station, and the ubiquitous women's association. The best will come last: we will go to the Panjshir Valley, Massoud's home base, and visit schools, a hospital, a displaced persons' camp, and another women's association. Then I will return home. All in a week! Looking back, it is hard to believe that such an agenda was even conceivable. In any case, another agenda awaits us. And for Nasrine, another life.

The Tajik plane is fitted with the narrowest seats and tightest spacing of any I have ever flown in. Despite the discomfort, my eyelids droop and I doze off. Hours later, we reach our Turkish stopover, and everyone stumbles out into the cold, dark night. I feel like a cow in a holding pen as we are herded into a huge, empty Istanbul airport terminal that lacks food services or places to sit. I wander around like a sleepwalker until we are herded back onto the plane.

It is still night—or night again—when we land in Dushanbe. An Afghan embassy representative together with our interpreter, eighteen-year-old Khusrow, a refugee from the Panjshir Valley, are there to meet us and take us to a hotel.

Before we go to sleep at 4:30 a.m., Tajik time, we arrange to be awakened at 9:30. When I hear the hotel floor attendant knock on the door, I rise and dress quickly, but Nasrine and Sara are still asleep. I go down to breakfast alone in the big, plush, Russian-style restaurant.

When we finally get together, we are driven to the Afghan embassy and begin to learn the hazards of travel in foreign countries where we don't know the rules. Each of us has only one entry visa for Tajikistan, and we used those visas when we entered the country the previous night. We will need another set of entry visas to get back into Dushanbe when we come back from Afghanistan. We should have realized that we didn't have visas for multiple entries, but somehow none of us did. All our plans for Dushanbe have to be scrapped while we scurry around trying to get our visas. We rush out, only to wait in offices all morning. I am frustrated, but recognize the moment as one of those serendipitous occasions that make each trip unique, plunging a traveler into the "real" life of a new country. The city opens up to me as we drive around and go in and out of offices. It seems a genial place, with wide boulevards, green trees, and a mild climate, its streets filled with healthy-looking, busy people.

The lovely government buildings are less lovely inside. The original large offices and even the marble corridors have been subdivided into dark warrens with ugly, mass-produced metal furniture and stacks of paper overflowing onto floors.

It is a long day of negotiating an unfamiliar bureaucracy, but a successful one—or so we think. When we return, at last, to the Afghan embassy, a translator informs us that we will also need a second set of exit visas from Tajikistan! Without them, we will not be able to board the plane for our trip home. During all our time that day with various officials, no one had seen fit to tell us this.

The news has just begun to sink in when Massoud's nephew, who is the defense attaché in Dushanbe, comes into the office to greet us. He looks remarkably like pictures of his uncle, with the same long, narrow face. "No problem!" He airily waves away our dilemma. "When you are due to leave, just pay a fee for another exit visa and that will be that."

But one crisis solved seems to activate another. A new official walks into the office almost immediately and reports that no planes can fly into Afghanistan until September 9, nearly two weeks away. We are flabbergasted. Has something terrible happened? No. It appears that Tajikistan is preparing to celebrate the tenth anniversary of its independence from the Soviet Union and has decided to close its border with Afghanistan. Could they fear an attack from the Taliban? We never find out, but the news is devastating for us. Nasrine and I go over and over my alternatives. Should I spend my week in Dushanbe and return home as scheduled without seeing Afghanistan? Or change my plans and my ticket, and wait with Nasrine and Sara until we can all enter the country? I quickly come to the only possible decision: I will go to Afghanistan.

But the roller coaster ride is not yet over. The defense attaché comes into the room with good news: We don't have to wait until the ninth after all. He has arranged for a van to pick us up early the next morning and drive us to Kalab, a small military air base that the President of Tajikistan, Emomali Rahmonov, has provided for Massoud's use. There, one of Massoud's helicopters will fly us to Khoja Bahauddin in Afghanistan, as planned. I am so relieved and happy that I cannot stop thanking him.

Finally, we relax. I am not entirely sorry that Nasrine's plans for Dushanbe are now impossible. I have spent years on official trips, trudging through tours of schools and hospitals and sitting through meetings with associations. I know they are important, informative, occasionally even moving—but I've had more than enough of them, and secretly I've come to dread them. I am delighted that instead I have a few hours to enjoy this charming city.

Dushanbe was created by the Soviets from a small provincial village and its population is now about five million. We are in the downtown, central district, which is crossed by wide boulevards bordered by full-grown shade trees. From a 1960s visit to Tashkent, Uzbekistan, as part of a peace delegation, I am familiar with the practice of digging gullies alongside many of the streets where fresh, clean water flows to cool the semitropical air. Streets are also cooled and cleaned by nightly wash downs. Wide, unbroken sidewalks are full of pedestrians, the majority of adult women wearing traditional dress: colorful, loose-fitting shifts patterned with a multicolored design of jagged stripes. College students are clustered around several schools. Buildings, freshly painted white for the anniversary celebration, are low, two or three storied, imparting a pleasant, provincial ambiance. Some public buildings mirror Washington, D.C.'s neoclassical style. Murals and mosaics on many buildings and fences add a colorful note.

During the night I wake to a turbulent thunderstorm and am fearful that we will not be able to leave, but I fall back asleep. At three in the morning I am awakened again, this time by Nasrine banging on the door. She has read her clock wrong and thinks it's time to get up. Again I drop off. Despite the bad night, we manage to be ready on time and leave the city at 6:30 on a clear and cool morning, accompanied by a man from the Afghan defense attaché's office.

The drive to the remote military air base takes three and a half hours. Outside the central city, Dushanbe's grand buildings disappear, replaced by the kind of makeshift housing found in impoverished areas that ring cities throughout the global South. The car climbs several high barren hills, passes rivers, and then goes by a sun-dashed blue lake spotted with miniscule rocky islets. As we descend into a valley of cotton plantations, the air gets hotter and hotter. Goats, turkeys, and geese roam freely in the villages. We pass orchards and vineyards, great swathes of wheat fields stretching to the horizon, and herds of cows and horses. Further south, the houses and walls are made of mud and straw, and there are acres of shining green rice. All this land belongs to the state, and the major crop, cotton, continues to be exported to textile factories in Russia. As part of Imperial Russia and then the Soviet Union, the Central Asian countries were exploited for their natural resources and cultivated as agricultural colonies. Much of that economy still prevails.

We drive into the small, sequestered Kalab airfield. I later learn that this rustic military base is the one the CIA has been using since the previous year, when, concerned about the Taliban's collaboration with Al Qaeda and bin Laden's terrorist training camps, they decided to establish contact with Massoud. CIA teams usually flew into Afghanistan on one of the rusting, patched-together M1-17 transport helicopters that Massoud kept at Kalab. Fearing they were risking agents' lives with every trip, headquarters sent a team of mechanics knowledgeable about Russian helicopters out to Kalab. Apparently, the mechanics were stunned that Massoud's men had managed to create functioning aircraft from Hind attack engines packed into the bays of M1-17 transports. They reported that the helicopters were "flying miracles," mismatched gum-and-baling-wire machines.

One of these flying miracles is standing on the tarmac when we arrive, its blades already rotating. The defense attaché's man is agitated. He quickly throws all our bags out of the trunk, helps us out of the car, then pulls us along, urging, "Hurry, hurry, please, the helicopter is waiting!" Nasrine is adamant that we're not going anywhere just yet. She insists that we have to change into our good clothes.

"Please, please, get on the helicopter," the Afghan begs.

But Nasrine whispers to me, "I think Massoud himself will be in Khoja Bahauddin. I think we will be able to interview him." She turns to the Afghan and says in a tone that allows no disagreement, "We must change our clothes."

He throws up his hands and leads us to a rugged outhouse several yards away, each of us dragging a piece of luggage. I pull out my one good outfit, a peacock blue silk shirt and pants that I brought for official occasions, and as I'm throwing the shirt over my head, I hear a terrible sound: the engine of the helicopter as it roars by over our heads. I peek out in time to see the Afghan shrug his shoulders, get back into the car, and drive off.

Nasrine, Sara, and I stand outside the shack, dumbfounded. In an instant, we have been stranded in this forlorn spot. I am sweating in my ridiculous tight silk outfit, anxious, and furious at Nasrine. But there is no time for recrimination. A group of heavyset, bearded men swagger over to us and demand our passports. At least Nasrine can communicate with them, since the Tajik language is closely related to Dari. Reluctantly, we take out our passports and hand them over. The Tajiks tell us that they are military border guards and we have to go through customs with them. It is now clear that this is what our Afghan friends had wanted us to avoid and why a helicopter had been ready to go the instant we arrived.

We follow the men over dusty, rocky paths, dragging our luggage with us, to an old train boxcar sitting in a field of weeds and desiccated trees. Hours of harassment commence, to the great amusement of a gaggle of soldiers hanging around for the show. Nasrine whispers that we are to say nothing, offer nothing, that she will do all the talking. Of course, Sara and I are incapable of contributing anything, since we don't speak Tajik. The two of us sit on rusted, rickety chairs and try to be as unobtrusive as possible. But Sara is young and pretty and the center of attention for all the men. She is petrified. I am mainly uncomfortable in my inappropriate silk in the intense heat.

Each of us is taken into the boxcar and interviewed, with Nasrine serving as translator. The head man keeps up a jocular tone as he comes on to Sara. When Nasrine realizes that they are essentially brigands, that what they really want is money, she regains a measure of confidence and negotiates a sum. Now that they have what they want, the men bring us to a low outbuilding and into a storeroom where we will spend the night. We have no idea when another helicopter will arrive and have no choice but to settle in and wait. At least this time, they've helped us drag our suitcases.

The room we are in is used by the local women who come daily to clean the offices and sleeping quarters of the crew. We pull together some army cots scattered around the room and lie down to rest, but our trials are not over. Sara is becoming ill; she turns feverish and begins to toss on her narrow cot. Fortunately, a small medical team, there to treat the soldiers, is housed across the hall. They kindly bring over some medication, and all three of us turn in for the night, after a "dinner" of tea and rice.

The next morning, after a breakfast of tea and nan, the ubiquitous bread of much of this region, Nasrine walks over to the base headquarters to see if she can find out anything. She comes back with the news that the Afghans know where we are and a representative will be with us later in the morning. Soon enough, an Afghan major under Massoud's command, who is resident in a nearby town, comes to meet with us. He is middle aged and looks so much like one of my uncles that I immediately feel comforted, certain that he will rescue us. Perhaps he will, but not right away, as it turns out. He says that Tajik security has learned about us, and the regional security chief has decided that we must immediately go to his office, nearly forty miles away. What can we do? We get into a car with the major and a Tajik security officer and head off.

The situation has made us testy—I more than Sara, who nurses her misery in silence. Nasrine drives me into a fit of exasperation by continually calling Tajik security the KGB. I retort that KGB is an outdated ex-Soviet term and inappropriate. We both sulk.

The security chief's office is a new building in the center of a small town. We are greeted cordially, and then a long discourse ensues between the Afghan major and the Tajik chief. According to Nasrine, the chief begins by claiming that no more helicopters are available and we will have to return to Dushanbe. The major insists that's not possible. The chief then says we do not have the correct documents; we should have gone to the Department of Labor—no, to the Department of Foreign Relations. It quickly becomes clear that here is someone else who wants something from us. Not money, it turns out. No, he wants the Afghan major to provide his men with fifty uniforms, so that they can make a good showing at the tenth-anniversary celebrations. Nasrine and I, friends again, feel terrible that we have brought this burden on the Afghans. But a bargain is struck, there are cordial handshakes all around, and we are driven back to spend another night at the grim base. This time, the base staff have decided to make us more comfortable, and a kitchen worker arrives with a dinner of borscht, salad, and melon. I eat nothing. I have begun to have stomach cramps, and the only latrine is a dark, stinking outhouse. I sip a little of my precious water and eat some candy, thinking about how rapidly my projected week is disappearing. I decide that once in Afghanistan, I must stay for an additional week.

The next morning dawns bright and hot. And what a morning it will be! Three helicopters are lined up on the field. Time passes, nothing is moving. What can go wrong now? Finally, Nasrine tramps over to the base headquarters to locate someone in charge. The message is that we will definitely leave that day. Determined that we will be ready this time, we drag our bags out to the field, as near to one of the helicopters as we can get, and sit down. The sun creeps across the sky, and there are no trees for shade, but we continue our vigil on the airfield, resolved that no helicopter will take off without us. Sara is passive; Nasrine and I pace, more and more anxious as the hours pass.

As we patrol the airfield, we have ample time to study the helicopters, which are small and battered, discarded Russian machines. Finally a pilot strides onto the field. Without bothering to acknowledge his passengers, he climbs into the nearest machine to fiddle with something. Then, frowning, he climbs out, peers under the aircraft, mutters what sound even to our ears like curses, and strides off the field. By this time several base workers are out on the tarmac with us, and to our nervous inquiries they reply that it appears the helicopter has a leaking gas tank and cannot be flown that morning. We lug our bags over to the next helicopter and, as our faces and arms redden from the sun, we wait again, and hope.

The pilot strides onto the field once more. We watch him closely. He walks around the second machine, kicks it in several places, bends to look over the tires. He mutters something.

Then he turns and walks over to the last helicopter. This time, as we pull frantically on our bags, the base workers join in and lift the heaviest. The pilot is on top of the machine, using a screwdriver to tighten the rotor blades. Then he waves to us to get in and climbs down.

We are so afraid of not being able to leave that we have lost all fear about our means of getting out. But at my age, actually climbing into the helicopter—without, of course, any of those portable steps—presents a whole new challenge. Our bags are thrown in, and Sara and Nasrine haul themselves aboard, but I am totally stymied. The workers prove to be real gents: while Nasrine and Sara pull at my arms from above, the men lift me from behind and shove.

I am gleeful on boarding the helicopter, until I see the interior: totally bare, no lining on the rusted metal body, no seat other than a single narrow metal bench along each side. The helicopter rises from the ground before I can catch my breath, however, and I sink down on the bench. There is nothing to hold on to as I twist around to look out of the round window.

It is wonderful, sensational. We float over ripe fields of green rice and golden wheat. We are flying so low that we can see everything beneath us in precise detail. Stands of trees, serving as windbreakers and demarcators, surround compounds of flat-roofed mud-brick houses, small orchards, and fields. We fly over a river with sandy shallow islets. It looks so peaceful, I am totally relaxed. I savor the view and the unworldly sensation of being above and yet so near. And then the helicopter sinks down and we land in a grassy field.

It is a scene I shall long remember. Nasrine, Sara, and I jump out of the helicopter. I watch my friend—cerebral, poised Nasrine—fling her arms wide to the sky, face shining, glowing with joy as she screams, "I am home, I am home!" She falls to her knees and kisses the ground.

We scarcely have time to look around—at the river on one side, at the sand-colored cliff, studded with mud dwellings, on the other—before a jeep hurtles down the cliff toward us, filled with young men, all dressed in clean, pressed, white shalwar kameez, the traditional male attire of baggy pants and long shirt. The driver is a handsome, slender, bearded young man who greets us formally. Another jeep drives down the embankment, and most of the men pile into it along with our bags, while we get into the first jeep and we all drive off.

We climb the cliff onto a dirt road, and then we seem to go back in time three thousand years, as we come upon a village, its sun-bleached white undulating walls winding down footpaths that shelter and hide family compounds, enclosing the empty road until it suddenly opens onto a large square with a single well in the center. Then the walls close in again, and the road leaves the village.

I am stunned, literally, by my reaction. Rising, inexplicably, out of some ancient Hebraic tribal archetype within my being, the image of this village resonates in my brain and in my soul. As in a dream, I feel as though a piece of me has always been a part of this place. I am spellbound as the jeep rushes on to the Northern Alliance compound.

Massoud's rearguard base in Khoja Bahauddin was built after the Taliban overran his former base in the town of Talaqon. Built on a bluff, the compound overlooks the Amu Dar'ya, the longest river in Central Asia, known in ancient times as the Oxus. The compound is divided into two sections. On the large side, the original simple concrete building consists of guest rooms and an office. There is also a small house further down the hill. In the other section there is a newly built residence for Massoud.

We are taken to the new section, and to our surprise we see, in this remote location, a white-plastered villa that looks like a small Mount Vernon. A wide, columned verandah surrounds the dwelling, which we enter through large French doors. Bisecting the one-story house is a hall through which I can see another set of French doors opening to a rear verandah.

I catch a quick glimpse of a large dining room and formal living room before we are led to a corner suite of two sitting rooms, each with two beds, and a large tiled bathroom. Shoukria, the founder of NEGAR, is waiting for us, worried over our delay, and we all embrace with affection and relief. She is winding up a trip escorting a group of French journalists and has delayed her return to Paris to wait for us. It is an honor, and a tribute to Shoukria, that we will be the first guests to stay in the new house.

During her years of traveling in and out of the northern provinces to organize among women, Shoukria has met many of the Northern Alliance men, including the young foreign ministry official, Assim Suhail, who is head of the Khoja Bahauddin compound. Assim is an ardent supporter of women's rights and provided support for NEGAR's meeting in Dushanbe the previous year. He is the one who has agreed to provide us with these relatively luxurious accommodations.

We have no time to unpack before we are called for our formal welcome. We pass through the gate in the wall that divides the new section from the rest of the compound and enter the stark, one-story, L-shaped building. There are five guest rooms, which are also used for meals, meetings, and socialization. The office is the only room that has more than the most basic furnishings; it even has a rug over the concrete floor. At one end of the room is a large mahogany desk and a tall cabinet that holds electronic equipment, although the only electricity in the compound, I learn, comes from a small generator used for a few hours each evening.

Six or eight young men, Assim's staff, are sitting in a circle on plastic chairs.

Assim and Nasrine exchange formal greetings, using English, of which Assim knows a little, and Sara and I are introduced. I give the usual spiel about women's rights and the Taliban and then I blurt out, "But you are all so young!" Assim, the oldest, is in his thirties. After twenty-three years of war, many of the original mujahidin have been killed, and Massoud is "the Old Man" at forty-eight. Assim laughs and answers, "It is good that we are young; we will be there to make the changes."

Like the others, Assim is of Tajik ethnicity, slender, of medium height, with thick curly hair, a short clipped beard, and a mustache. He is not exactly handsome but has a keen, intelligent face. The oldest son of a Kabul beekeeper, with four sisters and a brother, Assim finished university and then established an educational center for both men and women in Kabul, with an emphasis on computer technology. He left Kabul to join Massoud after the Taliban entered the city. He has not seen his family for five years, but his wife, who is not well, and their three children are located nearby in Tajikistan. Over the next few days, as a dust storm keeps us in Khoja Bahauddin, we spend a lot of time with Assim, and my affection for this intelligent, good man continues to grow.

The guest rooms are crammed with roughly constructed wooden beds and piled high with luggage and paraphernalia belonging to the visitors who are in this section of the compound. The two French journalists who came with Shoukria share a room. There is also a Russian journalist and his interpreter, as well as a few others we do not meet. These rooms will also serve as our dining room most days, with a space cleared in the middle of one while everyone sits on the floor. For our meals, the cook rolls out a plastic sheet and sets down platters piled with rice and bowls of stewed tomatoes, onion, okra, and sometimes eggplant. Platters of nan are passed around to be used as both plates and implements. Since I cannot easily get down on the floor because of spinal stenosis and arthritis, I usually sit on several mattresses or someone's bag. The kitchen is an open area, in the corner of the high wall that surrounds the compound. Its semblance of a roof is made of woven grass supported by stripped sapling poles. Cooking is done over a fire pit. The only other building in the compound is a concrete latrine and bathhouse.

That first evening, however, we eat in the villa, joined by Assim. Shoukria and Nasrine talk about the petition for the Declaration of the Essential Rights of Afghan Women, and Assim agrees to help with distribution in the region and to arrange clandestine distribution in Taliban-occupied territory.

Before bed, I shower with cold water in the tiled bathroom. I am no fan of cold showers, but that is all there is, and that night it feels wonderful as I luxuriously soap myself and stand for long moments, letting the water flow over my head and body. Back in the room I share with Sara, I pull the sheet over my head, and as I doze off, the pleasant drone of Dari from the adjoining room fills me with contentment. I am back in Afghanistan. A different Afghanistan, but still, Afghanistan.

Zahera and her daughter, Leila (1990)

Shakira, President Mohammad Najibullah, and Director,
All-Afghan Women's Council (1990)

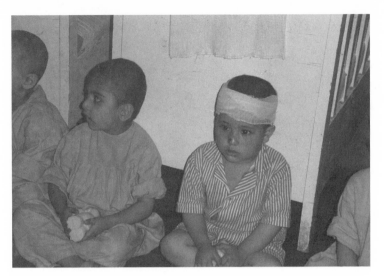

Babies' orphanage, Kabul (1990)

Khoja Bahauddin Guest House. Back row: Daood, Shoukria,
Assim, Massoum; front row: Sara and Nasrine (2001)

Girls' primary school at Khoja Bahauddin (2001)

Bick at the Qum Queshiaq internal refugee camp (2001)

Shoukria at camp mosque, with Nasrine on left (2001)

On the road from Khoja Bahauddin to Faizabad with
Mohammad Shreib (2001)

Road from Khoja Bahauddin to Faizabad (2001)

Rozstark market (2001)

Star Guest House, Nasrine getting petition signatures
from mujahidin, Faizabad (2001)

Mary MacMakin talking to
beggar, Faizabad (2001)

Bick with Mme Rabbani in courtyard of Rabbani residence,
Faizabad (2001)

Bringing Assim Suhail's coffin into Khoja Bahauddin compound,
Zubair leading (2001)

Bick, evening of September 9, 2001, Khoja Bahauddin

Afghan children gathering garbage during NEGAR's
Kabul conference (2003)

End of NEGAR conference; Zubair, center, conferring with
delegates (2003)

Chapter 4

Khoja Bahauddin

The next morning I awake with the dawn, too excited to remain in bed. While the others sleep, I go through the gate to the other side of the compound and stroll around, entranced by the sight of a wildly flourishing circular garden, an entangled medley of bright colors. I learn that it is the creation of an elderly mujahidin who lives nearby, and that once a week, a water truck lumbers into the compound to unload a stream of water into the garden.

The wall that surrounds the compound has two gates, one small, an entry to the villa and always locked, the other large enough for trucks, open all day, and guarded by a lone soldier on a rough wooden bench. I stand at the open gate and watch the traffic. The dirt road that runs past the compound is a major thoroughfare, busy throughout the day. First come a group of women, driving cattle to the river below us. A few of them wear burqas, but with the tops and front of the garment tossed back, leaving their faces uncovered and their hands free to work the cattle. Others wear long skirts and long-sleeved tops, and drape large scarves or shawls over their hair. Seeing a foreign woman visitor, they slow their pace to examine me curiously and I smile and wave. Their freedom to move about openly, to decide whether or not to cover themselves, makes a big impression on me, after everything that I have learned about life under the Taliban.

Next, several boys and girls ride by astride mules, with large water cans dangling against the animals' sides. The girls all seem beautiful to me, tanned and rosy, their long dark hair hanging loose and uncovered. Trucks also roar past, some farm, some military. Occasionally, a boy rides by on a battered bicycle; even more rarely, a motorcycle raises a whirl of dust.

When I go back to our rooms, Nasrine and Sara are awake. We soon learn that there are no helicopters available to take us to Faizabad right away. By this time, delays are nothing new to us. We are bordering a war zone in a part of the world where the rigid timetables of the industrialized world have no meaning. I tell Nasrine that I want to walk to the old village we passed on our way to the compound. "No, impossible! You can't leave this base!" she insists. This will be Nasrine's first reaction to all such requests, as her keen sense of responsibility for our welfare clashes with our desire for independence. But Sara also wants to see the area around the compound and has befriended a young man, Jaheen, who lives on the base and who will act as our escort and interpreter. He speaks rudimentary English and French, picked up from visiting guests, and has a quirky, happy-go-lucky personality. Nasrine reluctantly consents, and Sara, Jaheen, and I head off.

It is around eleven o'clock and the sun is high in the sky. The temperature is already in the upper nineties, but while intense, it is a dry heat, and not too uncomfortable.

We walk down to a bridge over the Amu Dar'ya, past laborers working on a new hospital on the bluff opposite the compound. Our side of the river is almost totally bare, hard-packed dirt with a few random, spindly trees; but, strangely, the other side is lush, with trees lining the bank and fertile green fields of rice. We stop to watch shirtless boys splashing and playing in the river alongside the mules and horses that stand passively in the cool water. The girls sit on their mules, watching the boys play. A group of women are in the shallow water near the bank, washing clothes while their children slosh and splatter around them. They stop their work when we pause to watch, and we all stare at each other for a few minutes before our group moves on.

We start to climb again as the sun blazes higher overhead. The air is getting hotter, and the hill steeper. "My friends and grandchildren should see me now," I think as I keep up with the pace.

We approach the mud walls of the old village I had been so moved by the day before. A young boy rides by on a donkey, long stalks of a plant wrapped in burlap hanging from both sides of the animal. A group of women suddenly stand before us, children clinging to their long, full, multicolored skirts. Most of the women have deep red-and-white patterned shawls covering their hair; several of them use the shawls to cover the lower parts of their faces, some seemingly out of shyness, others, possibly to hide their toothless mouths.

A few old men hobble over, and since the women hang back once the men approach, I ask Jaheen if he will ask the men some questions. We find out that they are displaced people who fled their villages as the Taliban militias advanced. The permanent residents of this village traditionally leave in the summer to work as itinerant farm laborers, so these people have moved into the empty houses and will have to go into a camp when the owners return.

We continue through the village, up one of the narrow lanes. More women begin to emerge from behind the walls. They stand at the openings of compounds to stare at us silently. Then some of them smile and beckon. We enter several homes, finding ourselves inside small compounds with tiny mud dwellings often built into one corner of the enclosing walls.

The village is still starkly beautiful, but it no longer moves me; instead I feel overwhelmed by the sparseness of the lives these women lead. Now, it seems one of the saddest places I have ever encountered. I have visited communities made up of boxcar or container dwellings, seen homes built of cast-off cardboard, lumber, and tin; yet they did not fill me with such a sense of desolation. Perhaps it is the silence, so heavy it seems to bear down on me, merging with the searing heat. Most villages, no matter how poor, carry the sounds of laughter, the tumult of children, radios blaring, whistles and horns, the drone of voices and sounds of labor. What was the silence of the ages yesterday, now seems the quiet desperation of war and upheaval.

Since these women have left villages where the Taliban has banned all music, I wonder if silence has become the norm for them, in this village of parched earth desiccated by the long drought of the past five years. Or is the silence a reflection of their exhaustion and the terrible circumstances of their lives? I truly have no comparable life experience with which to understand these women, and my sadness at their apparent blight leaves me emotionally and physically drained.

We enter the large center square that had been so mesmerizing the previous day. I slowly pace through the empty space, circle the center well, absorb the silence. Like the rest of the village, it simply feels sad. I am happy to have had that previous bewitching sensation, but I realize now that it was an ephemeral moment, perhaps emerging from the knowledge that in ancient times the Jewish people had lived in similar housing and environments. Indeed, an old legend has it that the Pashtun forebears were one of the lost tribes of Israel.

By now, my sadness, the sun, and the climb have exhausted me. I tell Sara and Jaheen that I am going back, and head off, taking a different path in the direction of our compound. I walk and walk through more of the village until finally I come to a new road and a group of buildings. A large sign reads: "ACT-ED—Agency for Technical Cooperation & Development. Emergency Assistance & Winter Emergency Shelter Operation for IDPs [internally displaced persons] North Afghanistan, Khoja Bahauddin. Financed by the Turkish People." I pause to study the sign, wishing that I might find one that reads: "Financed by the American People." But we Americans are too far removed physically and, for the most part, intellectually, from life in this tiny village. We lack information about the people, much less understand how our country has contributed to displacing the people I have just met.

I am now really tired. I can feel that my face is flushed with the heat and sun. I walk on until I hear a truck, at the sound of which I stick out my thumb, hoping it's a universal symbol. It works, or maybe it's just the sight of an elderly foreign woman standing by the side of the road, but the truck, filled with Afghan workers standing in the open back, stops and one of the men in the cab opens his door and helps me squeeze into the front seat. The truck drops me off at the compound entrance and, with all the workers waving and smiling, roars off. I cross over to the new villa, blissfully stand under the cold shower again, then fling myself naked onto the bed and sleep for hours.

We are tremendously privileged to be in the new villa, where we have privacy and a glamorous, modern bathroom. However, whenever we return to the compound from visits, we most often go over to the old side to meet other guests, whom we join for meals. The Northern Alliance puts up many visitors here, whom they hope will report to the outside world on the desperate conditions under which they battle Al Qaeda and the Taliban. Favorable reports will help bring forth critically needed funds and weapons.

Rabbani's government in Faizabad is recognized as the legitimate government of Afghanistan, rather than the Taliban in Kabul, by most of the international community including the UN. However, Massoud, the all-important defense minister, has transferred many of the ministries to Khodja Bahauddin, because he has long been unhappy with Rabbani's conduct as president during the 1992-94 civil unrest.

The compound has hosted warlords allied with Massoud; mullahs who oppose the extreme interpretation of sharia by the

Taliban; representatives from the UN, the World Bank, and the European Union; and international aid and health care agencies. During the few days that we are there, several journalists, representatives of various service agencies, and "goodwill" visitors such as us arrive. I meet one guest who speaks English. Everyone simply calls him "the Engineer," and he is ardently pro-Massoud. The only other women in the compound are two French journalists who have been traveling with Shoukria.

Nasrine, who speaks French as well as Dari, meets and converses with everyone. From her I learn that the Afghan visitors in the compound are all Muslims, but vehemently opposed to the Taliban. As a practicing Muslim, Nasrine feels comfortable with them; but she is also a strong feminist, which she publicly asserts by refusing to cover her hair. Like a growing number of Muslim feminists, Nasrine is committed to struggling for women's rights within Islam.

The strong link between all of Massoud's allies is that they revile the Taliban and its close ties with Pakistan, which they believe plans to exert its power over what would become a failed Afghan state. Afghanistan's lucrative drug and smuggling economy is said to be one of the lures for Pakistan. Equally important is the country's strategic position in relation to India.

One afternoon, I sit with Nasrine and Shoukria, Assim, and the Engineer, whose name, it turns out, is Kamal Nezaami. He owned a construction company in Kabul, which he abandoned after the Taliban arrived, and then worked in Pakistan. Kamal tells us that he has, completely on his own, developed a reconstruction plan for the region, with an astonishing four hundred projects mapped out. The war with the Soviets, the civil war, ongoing battles with the Taliban, plus the terrible drought, have heaped devastation upon devastation. Kamal has surveyed the locations of destroyed bridges, roads, irrigation channels, schools, hospitals, and other infrastructure necessary for economic restoration. He is anguished that he has the plans and the people who could do the work, but no funds.

The conversation shifts to the large number of women's associations in the region, and Shoukria wonders whether these groups could possibly help with reconstruction. Nasrine explodes with enthusiasm. "It's a fantastic idea," she cries out. "We can organize women in the States and they can adopt the women's associations here and provide them with funding and goods. We can get something really big started!"

"What are you talking about?" I blurt out. "Where are these US women? And who will organize them? Certainly not just you and me and the few others in NEGAR USA." I am really worried that the Afghans will take her seriously.

But Assim thinks I am questioning the existence of women's associations inside Afghanistan. He leaves the room and comes back with a map. Spreading it out, he sweeps his hand over most of the area north and west of Kabul. This, this, and this, he says, is under Northern Alliance control. Then he names towns and villages where there are women's associations.

"It's wonderful," I tell Assim, "that women are free to organize in your territory and it would be great if they can help with these projects. But I am sorry to say that it would be very, very hard to get many American women really involved." Nasrine nods glumly. I am truly unhappy to disappoint them. I know that there are a great many American women who are involved with local, national, and international projects, to address a multitude of needs, but I have had too much organizing experience to think that the few of us in NEGAR would have much success with a massive project such as this.

Nasrine suggests that I show Assim the photographs of my 1990 visit to Kabul. I have brought them with me in the hope that someone might recognize Shakira and Zahera, whom I still think about. Zahera's daughter, Leila, would now be seventeen years old. If they survived the fall of the Communist government and the chaos of the following years, they would now likely be living under the Taliban. I dream of rescuing them, of providing Leila with a college education. I never find anyone who knows them, but Assim does recognize the guerrilla leader, Feroza, who told us how she had organized the women of small villages to defend themselves.

"Oh, yes!" he nods. "I know who she is. She was a very famous fighter. Our enemy, certainly, but she did lead a band of women warriors."

I had never known whether to believe Feroza's story of being the commandant of seven thousand armed women who fought the "counterrevolutionaries," as she called the mujahidin, so Assim's confirmation elates me.

The next day, I have a private conversation with Assim about religion and the problems with state religion. Since I know Israel fairly well, I talk about the role of state religion there and the fact that Israel does not have a constitution to protect civil rights. The Orthodox have special status and privileges that are not available to other Israelis, which leads to endless internal tension. I know that Islam sees state and religion as unitary, but I remind Assim that there are secular Muslim states, such as Turkey, Morocco, and Tunisia. Both Assim and I, a Muslim and a Jew, are pleased to be talking like this. I'm particularly aware that we're having this discussion not far from the Taliban capital and the battlefields of their massing militia.

That same day, Assim informs us that Massoud is "supervising" our agenda, and that he hopes to meet with us. Assim also assures us that the helicopter that will be taking us to Faizabad should arrive soon. But not yet.

We decide to use our extra time in Khodja Bahauddin to visit a nearby school for displaced girls. We head off in the jeep with Zubair, Assim's assistant, and drive down a leveled gravel road that ends at a windswept plateau, empty except for the school. On a path of new concrete slabs, we walk past a neat, clean concrete latrine to the one-story school building. Constructed in a small U, it surrounds a tiny courtyard garden planted with grass and corn. The building holds four classrooms, a meeting room, and an office and serves between 160 and 200 girls each day, with twenty-five girls to a classroom and double sessions.

The girls are lovely, as most Afghan children seem to me. They have warm, taffy-colored skin, brilliant, large, dark eyes, and eager expressions. They are dressed in brightly colored loose dresses that fall to the floor. They remind me of children in eighteenth-century picture books, except for the headscarves they all wear. Some scarves are tied under the chin, some are tied behind, gypsy style; others are loosely draped over dark hair.

I want to embrace them all, but I also feel like weeping with the knowledge of how vulnerable they are. Something like a prayer keeps running through my mind, a prayer that somehow the means to safeguard these children will be found.

Although the girls sit three to a table, I am surprised at how well provided they are with supplies—textbooks, writing tablets, and abacuses. One class is learning numbers; another is working on art projects, and all the girls have colored pencils in cases. Nasrine talks to the children, asking them what they want to be when they grow up. All want to be teachers or doctors. We hand out candy to the delighted girls.

We sit down with the principal—a man—in his office. He has been a high school principal in a coed school and expresses great anger that in much of Afghanistan half of all children— the female half—cannot be educated. This little school teaches Islamic catechism, but as part of a larger academic program. It is a joint project of two nongovernmental groups, ACTED from Turkey and ECHO, the European Community Humanitarian Office.

Back at the compound, a new guest has arrived: Edward Girardet, an American resident in Switzerland, and a well-known foreign correspondent who writes for the *Christian Science Monitor* and *National Geographic*, among other publications. He has come with an interpreter, Mohammad Shreib, an Afghan exile who lives in Virginia. Ed had been in Afghanistan with the mujahidin many times during the war with the Soviets and was highly thought of for his dispatches and his powerful photographs. He has come to Khoja Bahauddin for an interview with Massoud. Although it is obvious that Massoud is not here, Ed plans to wait a few days in hope that he will arrive.

The next morning, I wake up much earlier than the others, as always, and stroll out to the rear verandah. Leaning on the balustrade, I glance down at a small house below. It is a segregated guesthouse for mullahs, uncontaminated by the presence of infidels. I heave a great sigh. Despite that jarring concept, I am so happy to be in Afghanistan. How fortunate I am to have this experience—a Jewish woman in this extraordinary Muslim country.

I sink into a chair and fall into a reverie. I dream that I am on a hill, in a white castle, and the handsome young mujahidin are princely knights gathered around King Massoud's Round Table. The peasants are all below. But—there is no Queen Guinevere! I sit up. Even though it has been obvious since the first day we arrived, it suddenly occurs to me that there is not a single Afghan woman in the compound. All the servants are men, the cooks are men, and certainly all the Northern Alliance staff are men. Of course, this is Massoud's northern base and a prime target for the Taliban so perhaps that is why there are no women around. Still, I am suddenly sobered. How will women ever become part of public life when they are isolated even from this more open resistance group?

Later that day we go for another visit, this time to a camp for the internally displaced that the French journalists traveling with Shoukria are eager to see. We are a large group: the French, two Arab journalists who are new guests, and Nasrine, Sara, Shoukria, and me. Zubair drives us to another high, barren plateau, where we come upon a village of tents. It is strikingly different from photographs I have seen of densely crowded refugee camps. The treeless plateau stretches to the horizon, and the tents are not cheek by jowl; here there is space, and sweeping vistas, a sense of openness, but also one of emptiness.

When we step out of the car, we are immediately surrounded by a group of ragged, unsmiling children and old men, many of them disabled, clothed in tattered kameez and turbans and, despite the heat, dog-eared jackets. One group of women stands apart, bunched in front of a few tents. Other women stand at the single well, silently watching us.

The men start speaking, almost shouting, torrents of words that, according to Nasrine and Shoukria, describe the horrors they suffered under the Taliban until they escaped from their villages. The men also complain that the world has forgotten Afghanistan, that the UN has abandoned them.These complaints seem almost a memorized litany to me. Nasrine tries to rapidly translate, but it is unnecessary. Their wails and their body language tell most of their stories.

I walk away. In Kabul in 1990, I had heard similar laments about the destruction, the tortures, the murders that people had suffered at the hands of the mujahidin. I have heard so many hideous stories about the viciousness, the loathsomeness of the Talibs; I know it is weak of me, but I just do not want to hear any more. So I walk away to observe more of the camp.

The most common shelters are shabby tents. Blankets are stacked in the rear to use in the cool nights and for the freezing winter to come. Rags tied to thin poles serve as walls or screens to separate one family's space from another's. The most wretched shelters are made of straw. Generally, straw is only for the flimsy huts that are used to store family belongings such as plastic tubs and buckets, iron cooking pots, and what look like more rags—but are surely the families' only clothing. Cooking is done in pits dug in front of the tents. I pass some deep pits that I guess are latrines. It is not just the stark poverty that is so grim but also the barrenness, which imparts a sense of despair.

We spend most of the afternoon at the camp, walking around, watching and listening as Nasrine and Shoukria speak to the people and translate for us. The sun is setting and the darkening sky shows the first stars of evening as we head back to the truck. Shoukria and Nasrine are moving slowly, finding it hard to leave without having been able to help in some way. They have vitamins and medicines and two hundred dollars to give to an administrative entity running the camp. But they have found no management, no camp committee. We are almost at the truck when Shoukria spies a strange construction. It is made of stripped-down tree branches covered with sheets and blankets, to form a tentlike room. Shoes are lined up outside, and inside we can see forty or fifty men kneeling on a grass floor mat.

"A mosque!" Shoukria crows.

She motions to Nasrine and me to follow her and strides into the makeshift mosque, walking straight through the rows of kneeling men. Shoukria has done the inadmissible! Not only are women not allowed to enter the area of a mosque where men are praying, but she is dressed as she always is: in pants and a shirt with a long beige silk scarf cascading from her neck. She never covers her mop of black hair. Nasrine and I are also in slacks, and have not covered our heads—much more of a problem for Nasrine than for me, but clearly all three of us have broken just about every rule there is about women's presence and behavior in a mosque.

Shoukria continues straight up to the front and stands before the group of mullahs sitting there. There is a stunned silence. The camp children and men who have been following us rush to peer inside. A woman has entered the mosque! A woman is demanding attention from the mullahs! Nasrine sits down on the ground and motions me to do the same. There is no way I can get down on the ground so I hunch over, trying to be inconspicuous—not very easy under the circumstances, but Shoukria begins to speak and everyone's attention shifts to her. First she addresses the mullahs. Then she turns to face the congregation. I cannot understand her words, but something about her rhythmic cadences reminds me of the great African American preachers of the civil rights movement. Shoukria spreads the dollars she has brought like a fan. She raises her arm in a commanding gesture. There are excited shouts and exclamations from the men. Nasrine begins translating for me.

First Shoukria asks the gathering, "Who are your leaders in the camp?" The men respond, "There are none." She asks, "Then who are the influential men among you?" The men shout and point out six men, "This one and this one."

Shoukria tells the men that we have brought money from the people of France and the people of the United States to help the camp. "This is your money," she says.

She turns to the mullahs and then back to the people. "I give this money to your mullahs," she declaims. "But it is not for them. They will keep it safe for you."

She lowers her voice. "You must work with your leaders. You must divide yourselves into six groups. Bring your women with you. Talk together about what the camp needs. What will make your lives here better. What will benefit your children. Then go to the mullahs with your leaders, and use this money wisely."

The sound of expelled breath from the massed men flows like a wave through the enclosure. It is dark inside the mosque. Dusk has passed into night. Blindly, I aim my camera in Shoukria's direction and click. The flash illuminates the scene for an instant and then I click the camera again. Miraculously, back in the States, I find that I have captured the dramatic scene.

Shoukria leads us out of the mosque and we walk quickly to the truck. As the truck pulls away, the three of us burst into excited shouts, "You see," Nasrine, once again the educator, tells us, "you see the genius of Shoukria's organizing. She has begun the process of transforming this dispirited, chaotic camp into a community." I believe, at that moment, in the possibility that Nasrine is right. My admiration for Shoukria overflows.

Two days have passed since our dramatic visit to the camp, and we are still unable to get to Faizabad. Sandstorms have made helicopter travel dangerous. A gritty haze fills the air, and the infrequent breezes have turned into a sharp wind. We decide that, despite the weather, we can wait no longer and will go by land. Ed has also decided to leave, since there has been no sign of Massoud. He suggests that we hire two vans and drive as a convoy as far as Faizabad, from where he will travel on to Kabul and then go home to Europe. The primitive roads are hazardous and we will be driving through desert, so Ed says it will be safer to travel with two vehicles in case one breaks down.

We all head by jeep into a nearby town to make arrangements for the vans, to place satellite phone calls to extend my ticket even longer than anticipated, and to alert Cindy that Sara will be traveling overland to Faizabad to interview Mary Mac-Makin.

The jeep pulls into a large, empty square, where a few staked saplings are bent double in the wind. Zubair stops before the first in a line of boxlike structures on a raised walkway above the dirt street. We clamber up onto the walkway—there are no steps—and go into a small store—nothing more than a recycled storage container. The young man who owns the store and the satellite phone sits on the floor near the open doorway. We pay him and place calls to the United States that go through quickly. Nasrine speaks to Max, her husband, and makes arrangements. I speak to one of my sons and send messages to the rest of the family. Sara's employer gives her approval.

We agree to leave at six the next morning. At 5:30, I get up, and walk over to the other side of the compound, where I find Mohammed Shreib standing beside two beat-up vans, the best they can find. We finally leave at 8:30, both vans piled high with all the luggage. We embrace Shoukria, who will be returning to France, and Assim, Zubair, and Jaheen, our constant companions. I have become particularly attached to Jaheen, who I have come to realize is wretchedly unhappy, ardent for an education, desperate to get out of war-torn Afghanistan and build a future for himself.

I am in the first van, in front, beside the driver, with Ed and Shreib in the back. As soon as we leave the township, the landscape becomes a wasteland, an eternity of dry, cracked earth. Sterile hills loom on the horizon. In a good year with enough rainfall, this land would have been rich with sweeping fields of grain, opulent with herds of braying cattle. We ride in silence, overwhelmed by the wretchedness of the scenery. Until the first breakdown.

The engine has been smoking for some distance. The driver jumps out and retrieves cans of water from the back. We wait as the engine cools down. It is obvious that the van has a leaking water tank. Ed curses softly under his breath. We haven't seen the second car since we left Khodja Bahauddin.

Apologetically, the driver tells Shreib that he will have to go to an auto shop when we reach the next town. We get back in, and the van chugs on. We are driving on caked earth with no visible road until suddenly we come up behind a dump truck pouring gravel onto the road, with a group of men raking it into place. Ed says the men are paid for their labor in grain, as are teachers, by the UN's World Food Programme.

This trip will change my thinking about many things, and prominent among them is my conception of the UN and its role in the world. Along with most Americans, I had half accepted the notion that it was not much more than an international debating society. But now I see firsthand the work of UN agencies like the World Food Programme and the children's fund, UNICEF, preventing hunger, providing homes, education, and jobs, and I become an ardent advocate of the organization.

Further along the new road, we are suddenly surrounded, as if by magic, by brilliant vegetation and palm trees. It is my first experience of an oasis town and it does seem miraculous. It is a market day and hundreds of villagers crowd the road, carting in vegetables to sell, hoping to buy staples for their homes. We pass donkeys loaded with straw-wrapped bundles that contain packed snow and ice, stored underground since the winter and insulated by the straw, that will now be used for refrigeration. Driving further into town, we circle a broad roundabout, in the middle of which is a luxuriant green park shaded by tall trees. Busy shops are all around. It is an astonishing transformation after the wretched empty miles we've traveled. Our driver lets us out on one of the wide streets feeding into the traffic circle and drives off to find an auto supply shop.

The curbs are lined with carpeted platforms on which men recline, drinking tea, eating grapes, and exchanging news. We settle onto one of the platforms, anticipating that we will see the second van when it arrives. Ed and Shreib call for tea and grapes. The great bunches of green grapes look luscious, and Ed claims they are the best in the world. Next to the platform sits a barrel of filthy water. Big black flies instantly cover the grapes. Ed and Shreib swish the grapes around in the foul water and happily eat them. I am aghast, and decline the offer to join them.

Kids stop to stare at a bareheaded woman sitting on a platform, chatting with the men beside her. When the numbers swell and block the street, local men shoo the children away. Another group quickly forms. Women never eat or visit with other women on the street. They never loiter when they go out to shop or to sell goods, so I am truly a spectacle.

None of the passing women wear burqas, but they cover their hair with scarves. The local female dress is black pants and blouse, with a long, colorful skirt over the pants. The skirts are made of the same brilliantly designed cloth as that of the men's skullcaps. I smile at the women, enchanted to see them dressed so colorfully and with individuality—more evidence that the Taliban's militantly enforced dress code is an aberration in Afghanistan. The women shyly smile back as they hurry past.

Several waiters, running up and down the steps of a building opposite, signal to us to come upstairs. We cross over and enter a large bare room, with a ring of twenty or thirty men settled on the floor, eating freshly roasted kabobs—and Nasrine, happily among them, deep in conversation. She is in her element, sitting on the floor with no head covering, all the men listening intently to what she is telling them. Somehow or other their van passed ours, perhaps taking a different rutted road into town. Nasrine's driver has spoken to ours and tells us that the van is still in the auto shop. It is midday, very hot, and Ed suggests that we all go to an NGO building he knows, assuring us that we will be welcome to wait there. We drive through streets with brick buildings and gardens until we come to the house, which belongs to Shelter Now, an evangelical Christian group, several of whose members were arrested in Kabul by the Taliban, accused of proselytizing. The group is very involved in humanitarian efforts and basic literacy teaching. We are indeed welcomed, and Sara and I promptly fall asleep in a quiet bedroom.

When we awake, the others tell us they have decided we must keep going even though our van is not fully repaired. Most of the distance to Faizabad is still ahead and it would be dangerous to travel after dark, not only in case of accidents but also because of brigands. So we set off, leaving the luxuriant greenery and human society of the oasis and enter the empty realm of scorched earth again. The vans quickly lose sight of one another and we are left to fend for ourselves. Ed's plan of having two vans in case one broke down has simply evaporated.

Occasionally we pass shepherds, their flocks inert under the shade of a lone tree. It is always a surprise when buildings emerge from the low hills. Men appear, seemingly from nowhere, and stand starkly silhouetted against the sun-bleached sky, watching us until we disappear. The terrain begins to rise. The ground, cliffs, farm buildings, as cracked and pitted as the hills—all are washed out by the sun until they look alike. Roads are barely differentiated from the stony earth. The driver frequently turns off into a dry river bed, easier to traverse than the rutted ghost of a road. Other times he drives through streams, splashing through the shallow but still rapid currents, water flying up through the windows. He always jumps out at the sight of water, fills his jugs, pours water into the tank. The overheating engine is a constant concern. Finally we leave the valley and spiral up narrow paths, over rocks and boulders, into low mountains of bare, jagged rock.

Back at Khoja Bahauddin they had told us that the drive would be rough, but this is worse than anything I could have imagined. I am bounced up and down and thrown sideways. My head hits the roof of the car. The hot wind blows through our open windows, bringing in gritty sand that collects on our clothes and exposed skin. My head is wrapped in a scarf, but the thin material seems to absorb the grit, and grains of sand penetrate to the root of each strand of my hair. Our van, rented for three hundred dollars for the day, is really a wreck, and our poor driver is just skin and bones. We cannot be angry with him; he is too pathetic. We just hope both he and the van will last long enough to get us to Faizabad.

I am terrified each time we drive on the roughly bound boards that serve as bridges over deep canyons. I clutch the seat, pulling my stomach and buttock muscles tight, as the van, screeching and creaking, slowly passes over dizzying heights. We come upon a deep, turbulent river rushing through the wasteland. Between sharp cliffs, the remnant of a great bridge made of rock and concrete crosses most of the river at a low point. But the end of the bridge no longer exists and a rough wooden platform connects to the other side. We make it over without crashing through, and our driver again jumps out and fills his water jugs, pours streams of water into the tank and over the engine. We continue to climb.

After another crossing of the same river, we come to a real highway; this and the few other highways like it in these formidable, rugged mountains were built by the Soviets for their tanks when they tried to subjugate the Afghans. I can't help but view these roads as one positive remnant of the Soviets' destructive passage through the country, despite the purpose they were built for.

We come upon a rustic roadhouse, built on a bluff overlooking the river. We park and I stumble out of the van. My weak legs are trembling. I hobble over to the steps built up the cliff and manage to climb slowly onto the open porch. I flop down at the table and am delighted to discover that the proprietor has bottled sodas. The view is spectacular—the soaring, jagged mountain peaks above and, below, the tumbling, rushing water.

I return to an earlier discussion I'd been having with Ed about the camp for displaced people. "I'm still haunted by the helplessness those people displayed," I say. "They seem to be just waiting for someone, for something, to come and help them. I have to say I found it irritating when they complained about being abandoned by the UN."

Ed works with the International Center for Humanitarian Reporting, and understands the refugee issue at all levels.

"The Afghan refugee problem is enormous. Some six million people have fled during the last twenty-three years—the largest number of refugees of any country in the world," Ed replies.

"But the camp we visited was for the internally displaced. They are in their own country. Why can't they use the great resource lying right at their feet?" I protest. "The river flowing below their camp. Why can't they carry water up to their camp? They could grow vegetables. They could plant trees—shade trees, fruit trees. They could even plant flowers just to put some color in their lives! I bet the Engineer could help them rig up a simple pumping device to bring river water up to the camp." I pause, a little ashamed of my outburst. There I am, a cosseted American, blaming people who have nothing.

"Ed, it's not that I don't understand that those men and women have gone through great hardship and misery," I say. "But is that enough to break their spirit forever? When do people lose their will, not just to survive, but to overcome?" I really need to know, and Ed has been to many camps.

"It's not just lack of will," he says. "When people have nothing, not even shovels, then everything has to be provided for them: tools, seeds, and sometimes someone with technical expertise. You need foreign countries and international agencies to sponsor the projects. Norway and Sweden work with the World Food Programme and pay workers with food."

I find myself near tears as I imagine the camp with trees and vegetable plots in front of the tents. I feel sure that with growing things around them, the women and men would begin to build homes instead of mere shelters. I am a little ashamed of my irritation with those hapless people, but I am also defensive and annoyed that I feel that way. Sobered by our conversation, we get back in the van, and head off. Miraculously, as it seems to me, by late afternoon we are approaching Faizabad.

Chapter 5
Faizabad

The day is still bright as we enter Faizabad. It is September 4. I had planned to be back home the following day, but instead I have finally arrived in this town of some one hundred thousand people, the administrative and commercial center of Badakhshan province and a good place to begin our investigation of women living under the Northern Alliance. Faizabad, an ancient provincial town, is set in a valley of the Pamir Mountains. The climate is moderate, although it can be snowbound in winter. Its fertile soil is bountiful, amply irrigated by the Kokcha River. During the Soviet invasion Faizabad was the site of a major garrison of some six thousand Russian troops.

As we drive through the hilly, crowded streets, we pass market districts where shops and street stalls display meats and fowl, stacks of produce, and clothing. We also pass through an industrial area filled with piles of used building materials. Our car descends a steep incline leading to a concrete embankment that confines the thrashing, white-capped Kokcha. Rock cliffs loom on either shore. The road follows the river for a short distance, then ends abruptly at a concrete causeway that leads to a flat rock in the middle of the river. We walk across the causeway to a low building—Star House, another Northern Alliance guesthouse. The river beats against the rock on all sides, but the stur-

dy house sits stolidly on its rampart, impervious to the force of
the dashing waves. What a wonderful contrast it is to the guesthouse on the sun-scorched mesa of Khoja Bahauddin!

Once again, Nasrine and Sara have arrived before us. Nasrine stands at the end of the causeway, beaming and calling out,
"Come in, come in." She eagerly pulls me up the steps. A tall
woman with a broad smile stands beside Nasrine. She looks
amazingly like Eleanor Roosevelt. It is Mary MacMakin, the
American whom Sara has come to film.

Mary has been in Faizabad for several days, anxious to meet
us, wondering why we haven't arrived sooner. Our bags are put
into a small room at one end of the building and we quickly go
to join Ed, Shreib, and several Afghans in a large dining room
for a dinner of nan, rice, meat, vegetables, and tea. At the end of
that long day, I just want to relax, so I tune out the conversa-
tional din and concentrate on the dining room. It is furnished
with the same carved, gold-painted furniture as in the villa at
Khoja Bahauddin. Gauze drapes, gently stirred by breezes from
the river below, frame wide French windows.

When we return to our rooms that first night, we realize
that the guesthouse is, like the one at Khoja Bahauddin, only lit
for a few hours each evening using its own generator. During
the night there are kerosene lanterns, and the long narrow hall-
way is lit by a single lantern on the floor, casting a ghostly waver-
ing light. I am a bit scared that first night, going down the hall
in that flickering light to the bathroom, where there is no running water. I flush the toilet with ladles of river water kept in a
large container and brush my teeth with a few miserly sips of my
bottled water. I have been given a nice room to myself across the
hall from Nasrine and Sara, with a window on each of the two
corner walls, both looking out on the rushing, glittering river
below. A large old sofa and coffee table sit beside the high double bed, which is stacked with half a dozen mattresses, blankets,
and coverlets. Since it is doubtful the coverings have ever been
washed, I take Nasrine's suggestion to spread my bedroll on top

and wrap myself in that. I keep the windows open for the river to cool and freshen the air.

The next day Ed and Shreib leave for Kabul and we head off early with Mary. We get into a car provided by the Northern Alliance and the driver slowly makes his way through narrow streets clogged with both animal-drawn and motorized vehicles.

When the Taliban decreed that girls could not go to school, education became a major issue and focal point for anti-Taliban groups back in the States, so we have decided that our first stop will be a high school for girls. The school is in a small stone building, identical to all the others lining the street. Above the doorway are two signs, one in Dari and the other in English, with a UN insignia above it: "World Food Programme. Food for Education Project. Norwegian Afghanistan Committee." The high school, founded in 1924, is quite famous and boasts fifty-eight teachers, eleven teacher assistants, four teachers with advanced degrees, and five administrators. All the teachers are women; the principal is—once again—male. The classes are taught in three shifts.

Entering the school through curtained double doors, we come into a small courtyard surrounded by whitewashed concrete classrooms, shaded by two ancient trees. Several teachers hurry out to greet us and bring us to their classes. The condition of the rooms is dreadful—cracked, discolored walls, desks made of rough planks worse than those used for vegetable crates in the States. Two or three girls sit on each bench. We enter another classroom where there is no furniture at all; the young women sit on the floor, each on her personal, colorful mat.

The girls are in their late teens. Their ethnic mix parallels that of the region: a majority Aryan, an ancient Persian group, and many Tajiks. The girls look healthy, alert, and poised in uniforms of long, lightweight black coats and white headscarves. Nasrine is glowing as she tells them in Dari, and us in English, that she wore the same uniform at the girls' high school in Kabul that she attended in the 1960s. I notice that many students have polished nails, rings, and watches and wear low-heeled pumps or sandals. Their white scarves are worn loosely back on their heads. Not too far from here the Taliban prohibits women from exposing their hair, hands, ankles, and feet.

The school has an academic curriculum: mathematics, sciences, social science, art, and languages. It also has an indoor sports and gymnastics program. It is tuition free, and UNICEF provides most of the textbooks. The teachers receive 49 kilos of wheat and 12.5 kilos of bottled oil a month from the World Food Programme, since they and their families can barely subsist on the government's miniscule and irregularly paid salaries. Despite the condition of the classrooms and the scarcity of school supplies, all the teachers comment on how eager the girls are to learn. "Their morale is so high!" is the refrain.

When this session of classes ends and the students are dismissed, we follow them into the courtyard and stand aghast as these beautiful young women pull blue burqas out of their bags and drop them over their heads. The girls become anonymous phantoms as they slip out of the gate and disperse down the street. My heart constricts. "Why do girls have to cover themselves in the heartland of the Northern Alliance?" we ask repeatedly. The standard explanation is that it is for protection. Just as during my visit in 1990, when we were unable to leave Kabul because, we were told, the borders were "porous" and enemies could be anywhere, we are told here that the area is porous and enemy agents may sneak into town.

On the following day, we visit a large hospital with buildings scattered over an extensive campus. Men and women wait in groups, some sitting on the ground under trees. The women all wear burqas but with the tops pushed back to uncover their faces. Most women are carrying babies. I am impressed with the comprehensiveness of the hospital: there are signs listing an emergency room, a blood bank, a pharmacy, a school of nursing, and a radiology department.

The Mother and Child Care Center is a two-story contemporary building. We meet with the director, who speaks English and received her medical degree in Kabul in 1984. She tells us that the hospital, founded more than thirty years ago with only twenty beds, has expanded dramatically; the surgical unit alone has twenty-five doctors, eleven of them women. The hospital has fifty nurses, eighteen of whom are women, all graduates of the local nursing school, and a pre-and-postnatal clinic is headed by a female doctor. The director emphasizes that there is no lack of competent personnel, despite low salaries, but laments that in every material way the hospital is deficient—they need equipment, supplies, and medication. I ask her about psychiatric care, remembering the facility I visited in Kabul. There is no longer a psychiatric facility anywhere in Afghanistan, she tells me.

The director's pride is evident as she tells us they have the only family planning facility in all of Afghanistan, which Doctors Without Borders helped set up three years earlier. Amazingly, abortions can be performed legally, although only for "therapeutic" or "medically needed" reasons. Doctors Without Borders also supports the hospital with outpatient medication for tuberculosis and malaria and with lab work and radiology. The World Food Programme helps with food for the patients.

On the third day, we include a visit to the regional UNICEF office, where we meet a young woman, Fauzia, who helps run the office. She is lovely, with a stylish haircut and an elegant loose silk dress that is both modest and fashionable. The habitual Muslim scarf is tied loosely around her neck. Fauzia tells us that she began medical studies at Kabul University but left when the Taliban closed all the schools. She is nearly fluent in English and lets us know that no women are included in the regular meetings of the nongovernmental aid organizations that coordinate local programs. Fauzia begins to describe a pet idea of hers, to set up a silkworm industry, when the UNICEF chief comes in and takes over. We are annoyed with the chief's discourtesy in treating Fauzia so dismissively, so we deliberately turn and direct a number of our questions to her. He answers in her stead however and, since it is clear that Fauzia wants to avoid conflict, we listen quietly to what he has to say.

UNICEF had programs all over Afghanistan, the chief tells us, but these are all closed in the areas conquered by the Taliban. Under UN rules they are not allowed to support schools that deny education by gender, so it is only in the north that UNICEF currently funds schools, some 250 of them. In addition, the Swedish Committee for Afghanistan provides aid to nearly 600 more schools. As is traditional in provincial areas, the schools are separated by gender, but both girls' and boys' schools are academic.

After all our excursions, we return to Star House to have our meals and relax. One day, three local women come to meet with Nasrine, who asks me to join them. Their political group has gotten the news that an Afghan woman activist from the West is in town, and these three have been delegated to meet her. The women appear to be poor, working class, meagerly dressed. They look worn and tired, but they are totally rapt as Nasrine speaks. They know Assim from Taloqan, their hometown, where Massoud was based before the city was taken by the Taliban. They tell Nasrine they love Assim and praise him for helping them get their group organized. I am thrilled to know that such groups exist, as they could be the backbone of a strong political movement for change. Nasrine is terrific, encouraging their political work, telling them about Western feminists, and explaining NEGAR's work. The women promise to get thousands of signatures for the petition from men and women alike.

Nasrine is eloquent and persuasive everywhere she goes, and she is tireless. When there are no guests available for her to proselytize at Star House, she sits outside and engages the mujahidin guards. One night she bursts into my room waving a petition with the signature of a prominent mullah who is an overnight guest.

In between our trips and meetings around Faizabad, I spend a good deal of time talking to Mary MacMakin. Sometimes, Sara turns the camera on while I "interview" Mary for the documentary. Her stories of life in Kabul before the Russian war and during the mujahidin civil war fascinate me. Mary came to Afghanistan with her husband and their four young children in 1961 when her husband, like hundreds of others from the developed world, was sent to help build Afghanistan's infrastructure. Bob MacMakin was commissioned by the Asia Foundation to develop an educational press. Mary describes the times as "just so much fun." Zahir Shah was an enlightened monarch. The city and countryside were unmarred by pollution or war. Afghan Islam was tolerant, diverse religions practiced their faiths, and foreigners took little notice of the problems underlying the calm exterior. Mary admits that in those days she wasn't necessarily aware of the tribal, conservative culture that was so oppressive to the overwhelming majority of Afghan women. She and her family spent six years living an idyllic, expatriate life in Kabul. They returned to the States in 1967. Four years later, Mary decided to come back to Afghanistan, leaving behind Bob and their now-grown children.

For ten years she lived the life of a Kabuli. A physical therapist, Mary practiced her profession and trained students in hospitals in Kabul and Taloqan. She left again in 1981, two years after the Soviets invaded, and returned in 1992, with the fall of the Afghan Communist regime. By then Kabul was a far different city from the one she had left eleven years before. The population was swollen with people fleeing the devastated countryside. Streets were filled with the wounded and disabled, with orphans and destitute widows.

"Still, the coming of the mujahidin government did not interrupt the normal flow of life in Kabul," Mary says. "Women continued to hold 80 percent of the teaching positions in Kabul's schools, young women as well as men attended the university, women worked in the post office, in government ministries, as flight attendants on Arianna airlines, with foreign nongovernmental and UN agencies." She is describing life in Kabul as I saw it in 1990 before the mujahidin came to power.

But as the rivalries and tensions grew within the mujahidin coalition, "It all fell apart" says Mary. She started an organization named PARSA (Physiotherapy and Rehabilitation Support for Afghanistan) to provide war widows with viable skills so they could support themselves and their families. Bob, who had retired to Bisbee, Arizona, became treasurer of PARSA, which was chartered in the United States, and editor of a newsletter to keep supporters informed on Mary's projects. One of the projects, a handicraft business begun in 1992 that sold items made by women to outlets in Kabul, the United States, and Canada, was still in operation in 2001. "We were even making and selling sanitary napkins," Mary says, "for the new spenders in town, the young women working for foreign agencies with a good salary, able to afford our product." Mary also set up job training for boys who were supporting their families.

But as the mujahidin infighting intensified, life in Kabul became a nightmare. "Hekmatyar wasn't able to seize control of Kabul for himself, so he started destroying the city block by block," Mary tells Sara and me. "He was safe in his nest ten miles away in Char Asyab, and he rained down rockets on the city, killing civilians by the thousands for a year and a half. The fighting got dirty as different ethnic groups battled each other. Then the rape stories started. A Hazara woman confirmed that she had been raped, after which gossip swept the city faster than e-mails, doubling, tripling the number of rapes. There may have been ten, there may have been five hundred rapes, no one knows; the assumption is that mujahidin from all the forces were raping, looting, and fighting. Women and girls stayed at home to be protected by their families.

"And then, in the winter of 1995-96, the Taliban militia pulled up close to Kabul and did the same blanket rocketing as Hekmatyar had earlier. For eight months they pounded the city, killing thousands more civilians, until the end of September, when Massoud moved his troops and armaments up to Jabal Seraj, forty-five miles away, at the foot of the Hindu Kush."

Mary witnessed what few Westerners had seen. "The Taliban rolled into town on a Thursday as Massoud's people pulled out. Friday was very quiet, the day for rest and prayers. On Saturday not a woman in all of Kabul went to her job, not a teacher, not a clerk. Out of the fifty or so desks in the huge Mille Bank, all but a handful were empty—just a few male clerks were there. Aid organizations and UN agencies were scrambling to run their offices without their female staff. The post office was in disarray as most of the clerks were women . . ." Mary stops talking, too upset to go on. She has lived through the past eight years of the Taliban's rule, seeing the women of Kabul turn into wraiths, unable to feed their children or themselves if they have no male relative to support them, locked away in their homes, barred from the most basic of human interactions. PARSA has helped some of them, but Mary has spent these years all too aware of the many women she cannot reach.

Although Afghan women were severely restricted, Mary was able to continue her public life as before, riding her bicycle, gray hair uncovered, seemingly just an eccentric elderly Western woman. But part of her life went underground; she set up covert schools for girls and managed to keep women working in her projects, despite the Taliban's decree that all Western agencies lay off all Afghan women on their staffs. In July of 2000, the Ministry for Prevention of Vice and Promotion of Virtue raided the PARSA office. Mary and her entire staff of men and women were carted away to jail, based on the claim that incriminating material had been found in Mary's possession. There was a major uproar among nongovernmental agencies in Kabul and in the Western media, which forced the Taliban to offer to release Mary and some of the men on PARSA's staff. Mary refused to leave the jail unless the seven women staff members were also released. Once they were all out, her visa was revoked and she was told she had to leave the country. She moved to Pakistan and set up her PARSA office there.

Mary dislikes working from Pakistan and she is planning to move her organization to the Northern Alliance's stronghold in Faizabad, so we get to see more of the town as we accompany her on her search for housing. One day Sara and I go with her to look at two houses for rent near the UN guesthouse where she is staying. This is a newer, planned district where streets are more or less straight, with two lanes of traffic. Pedestrian walkways are also straighter and broader than in our part of town, but they are still made of packed dirt, with flowing canal ditches alongside. The compounds are larger, built for prosperous families. After the Taliban banned Afghan women from working, many international and nongovernmental agencies moved their offices north to Faizabad so they could hire women, and most of the agencies are located in this newer district. Foreign agencies often have staff living quarters and guest rooms as well as offices in their compounds.

The first house is shown to us by the owner, a well-dressed, youthful woman bedecked in gold jewelry. She and her husband, a doctor, live elsewhere and rent this inherited, mud-brick house. It is on one side of the lot, while on the other side the compound boasts a vegetable garden and fruit trees. There is a separate building for a semi-open kitchen with an adobe oven, and another for the outhouse. A covered trough from the outhouse carries the waste to drainage beyond the walls. Water is delivered once a week to a cistern.

The house has several rooms, all without doors. Window openings are cut in the wall, but there is neither glass nor screens. The interior walls are mud, the floors hard-packed earth. Mary walks around as she considers how to use each room—one for her bedroom, one or two for staff and work space. A family is living there and they watch us despondently; they know a foreigner will bring higher rent and they will have to leave.

All this occurs while our meetings proceed relentlessly. The most interesting are with women community organizers and with President Rabbani and his wife.

The community organizers are four professional women who represent the Badakhshan Women's Association, formed in 1998 for the purpose of finding and creating jobs for poor women in the province. The group began with forty women, whose first project was a needs survey. They went into each of the sixty quarters, or neighborhoods, of Faizabad and in each met with a local woman who knew her community, its labor skills, and needs. These sixty community women agreed to be the core group that would meet regularly with the women of their neighborhoods on issues such as health care, hygiene, and family planning. I can hardly believe the level of work and sophistication of these women who have never been trained in this kind of organizing.

We visit one of the group's projects, begun with a grant from the World Food Programme, which provides the eighteen women involved with a kilo of wheat daily. The women are making a delicious candy, which is always available at Star House. We watch the hard, tedious, completely unmechanized work. Apricot pits are cracked open and the fingernail-sized nut inside pulled out. Meanwhile, sugar is being liquified in pans set over open fire pits. Then, as the apricot nuts are rolled and tossed in a large, heavy metal pot by one woman, another pours the hot sugar from a ladle until all the nuts are encased in a glistening white coating.

The four women who lead the association exemplify the type of educated middle- and upper-class Afghan women who have a long history of participation in voluntary groups. I wonder about the women we are meeting, the doctors, the teachers, and others in senior positions. Almost all did their undergraduate and graduate work at Kabul University under the Communist regime. I want to question them about how much they were influenced by the expanded role of women during that period, but I feel unable to ask Nasrine to translate such questions. I am surely being oversensitive, but I know her hostility to the Communists and I fear embarrassing her.

An elated Nasrine also manages to arrange our visit with President Rabbani. For the political leader of the Northern Alliance, I dress in my peacock blue silk outfit once again, the one I had brought along for such formal occasions, and Nasrine puts on her good black suit, with long sleeves and a skirt almost to her ankles. But she refuses to cover her long hair.

The headquarters of the Islamic State of Afghanistan is an old mansion. The green, white, and black national flag flies in front. Mujahidin stand, sit, and mill around outside.

In a long, marble-floored "throne room," we are introduced to President Rabbani, who wears a long white robe, an oversized gray silk jacket, and an elegant white turban. He is seated on a gold brocade divan with an elaborate carved back. Nasrine bows her head slightly to him and then presents him with copies of her two books, which he accepts with a warm smile. He knew Nasrine's family many years ago.

Mary, Sara, and I sit down on a row of straight-backed gold chairs opposite Rabbani; Nasrine joins us and then the president begins to speak in Dari. He talks. And he talks. He smiles. And he talks. My head keeps snapping up as I try to stay awake, but I can't help but doze off. Finally he stops, and Nasrine goes up to talk to him privately. Later, she tells us she asked him why women in Faizabad are wearing the burqa. He replied that he had never said they must. So Nasrine suggested that he encourage some of the older women to appear in public without the burqa. She feels optimistic that he will take up her plan for women to go uncovered. When the audience is over, we are told that we will lunch with Mme Rabbani at the family's home.

Enclosed by the usual high walls, the Rabbani's house resembles millions of middle-class dwellings in the United States, but looms large and luxurious in this old town. The front garden is overwhelmed by a huge circular satellite dish and towering florescent stanchion. A group of women, whom I think of as "a bevy of handmaidens," ushers us into a large room suitable for formal receptions. Then Mme Rabbani comes in and the room is transformed into a family room by her friendly presence. She is a large woman, forty-five years old, and she speaks to us in English.

We exchange gifts, which we always carry with us for unexpected moments such as this. We chat about our families. Both her family and her husband's have lived in Faizabad for generations. Her father, a judge, served in Parliament, and she graduated from the girls' high school we visited. "I used to be beautiful," she tells us laughing, "but after twenty years of war, I am no longer. First the Russians"—she casts her eyes up—"and now these silly ones. How did they descend upon us? They came and took away all the rights of women. This area is very freedom loving and my husband has a free mentality."

We know that, as a youth, her husband went to an Islamic university in Cairo, where he joined the conservative Muslim Brotherhood. Returning to Faizabad, he built a boys' religious school next to his house. Nasrine and Mary have both told us that, unlike Massoud, Rabbani is a traditionalist and has never, in his long career as a theology professor and Islamist party builder, shown any sign of concern for women's rights.

Nasrine leads the conversation around to the status of women and the wrecking of Afghan society by the Taliban. She explains the formation of NEGAR, the Declaration of the Essential Rights of Afghan Women, and our petition project to obtain a million signatures for the UN. As usual, Nasrine is eloquent, and Mme Rabbani responds with enthusiasm.

"I will get hundreds of signatures," she promises, "and will send them with my husband, who, as president of Afghanistan, will be going to address the UN in New York in November."

"Why don't you go to the United States with him?" I burst out. "We'll organize a large New York reception for you. We'll bring together the Afghan community, all the Afghan expatriates, with American feminists." Compared to some of the plans

Nasrine has put forth on this trip, I know organizing an event for Mme Rabbani would be a cakewalk. Rabbani is, after all, the UN-accredited President of Afghanistan, and few among the expat Afghan community are supportive of the Taliban. "We'll make it an evening to support your orphanage," I promise. Mme Rabbani seems to be considering the possibility.

Eventually we are called in to lunch, and gasp at the size of the freshly baked nan, as huge as the platter they are stacked on. There is rice cooked with pistachio nuts and raisins, a mound of roasted meat decorated with caramelized carrot sticks, bowls of eggplant and yogurt, a succulent roasted chicken, and more vegetable dishes. Dessert is milk pudding and a spread of fruits. Mme Rabbani clearly relishes a good meal, as indicated by her figure.

She wants us to see her favorite project, the orphanage and school we have promised to raise money for when—or if—she comes to New York. As we walk out of the house, she starts to slip on a burqa. Nasrine stops her and suggests that, as the wife of the president, she will set an important example if she walks with us with only a scarf covering her head. With a wide smile, Mme Rabbani looks over at her female entourage already covered in burqas for the outside and then, with her burqa thrown back on her head, she walks through the gate with us, her face uncovered.

As we walk along the street, Mme Rabbani tells Nasrine that Afghan women feel safer concealed under the burqa, given that the Taliban is so close and many of the people who have fled to the town are conservative. In Sheghnan, a more secure spot further north, near Tajikistan, where there are fewer displaced people, many women do not wear the burqa, she says.

We are in old Faizabad, which still feels very much like a village. Narrow canals, babbling like country brooks, run down the side of each street. We walk along dirt paths bordered by high walls and surrounded by greenery—wildflowers and grasses, emerald green moss and verdant creepers, grow alongside the blue water in the ditches, while bushes and trees reach over the walls to shade the paths.

Mme Rabbani's school and orphanage are housed in modern buildings. Women in long, multicolored dresses and wide shawls, as well as a row of children, are lined up waiting to welcome us. The school was founded as a residential establishment for both boy and girl orphans, but the years of war have created many homeless widows so the orphanage now houses thirty or forty of those with children, the women working as resident caretakers, nurses, cooks, and teachers. We spend six hours in the school and see dozens of children, ranging from babies to teenagers, in nurseries and classes, both academic and industrial. Mme Rabbani is charming and gracious, revered in Faizabad as a kind of noblewoman for her good works.

Back at Star House, I ask Nasrine what she thinks of the president. "He is not well liked," she admits. "Relations between Rabbani and Massoud are no longer close." Nasrine believes that Massoud has developed into a humane, thoughtful, and battle-weary warrior who has learned the lessons of compromise and reconciliation. Rabbani spent the war in Peshawar, as did most of the other mujahidin leaders, embedded with Pakistan's ISI. She suggests he has changed little over the years.

Our last visit in Faizabad is to a former student of Mary's. The woman is married to a local farmer, so the trip will give us an opportunity to visit a country family. Our driver slowly heads out of town, then onto a broad new road, which leads into an area of flat land, subdivided into building lots for a new suburb. A few new shops and houses are already built near the road. We soon pass into actual farmland. The Kokcha River here is a wide, calmly flowing, light blue body of water. Rich parcels of land, separated by mud walls, are heavily planted with corn, vegetables, and fruit trees. Across the river, above a bank of buff-colored rock, yellow fields extend to a distant horizon of rounded mauve hills. As we drive deeper into the countryside, large fields of grain, corn, and tall brilliant sunflowers stretch

down to the river, where there are still some light tents or
thatch-roofed structures that farm families use in the summer
for relief from the heat. Women are working in the fields and
tending to household chores. For the first time since we have
arrived, I feel a sense of tranquillity and appreciate the genu-
inely singular beauty of Afghanistan.

We come to a village, get out and walk through damp fields
to the farmhouse where Mary's student, Soraya, lives. Soraya
had been a widow when she attended Mary's physical therapy
class. Intelligent and outgoing, she enjoyed working but wanted
to get married again, even though the man she was interested in
had a first wife.

The village grapevine has sent her news of our arrival and
Soraya is already outside to welcome us. She leads us into a
comfortably-sized room, where we all—even I—sit on the mat-
covered floor, since there is no Western-style furniture. Soraya
is an amply endowed woman with an animated personality. She
is a picture of female fertility, with one baby at her bursting
breast, smelling of milk, and several toddlers and young children surrounding her. Shortly, the first wife, whose name I
never learn, walks in, demurely greets us, and joins us on the
floor. I am surprised that she is about the same age as Soraya,
but otherwise they are unalike in every way. She is slim, shy, and
quiet. Her two boys, about ten and twelve, stand behind her,
and she keeps her arm around her six-year-old daughter. We
are told that the first wife suffers from cerebral malaria, a particularly horrific manifestation of the disease that can cause sei-
zures and brain damage.

The first wife seemingly carries the burden of housekeep-
ing, while Soraya, even with her large brood, works as head
teacher in the large school in the village. Despite the teaching
and the children, Soraya jumps at the suggestion that she com-
mute to Faizabad and work with Mary to set up and run a physical therapy unit and training program at the hospital.

The first wife gets up after a short time and leaves the room with her children. She returns, and while her children spread a cloth on the floor, she puts trays of tea and fruits before us. Then she sits down and joins us again. I don't see overt hostility between her and Soraya. Her children are older, so that a natural kind of childcare takes place between them and Soraya's babies. The arrangement certainly seems to work for Soraya, but I can't help wondering how this first wife and her children feel about it.

From my one snapshot view of this farming village, life under the Northern Alliance seems to be essentially as it has been for generations. Boys and girls receive an elementary education, and women work as teachers, farmers, professionals, wives, and mothers.

I feel very positive about the Northern Alliance after this visit to Faizabad. We have seen a limited number of schools, but schools for girls do exist in the north and, despite extremely limited materials, children are being educated. We will also be able to report that women are working in many capacities, despite the traditional expectation that they remain in the home.

Within towns almost all women are covered by the burqa when they go outdoors, but in every workplace we have visited—hospitals, offices, schools, food production in town or on farms—women wear conventional Afghan clothing of long skirts and long-sleeved blouses, with headscarves. I understand that in many areas of Afghanistan, burqas have historically been a normal part of a woman's wardrobe, although not mandated as compulsory attire. Nasrine tells us that her mother used to pull on her burqa to shop for food on a bad-hair day.

It is September 8. All of us, including Mary, who will be going with us to Khoja Bahauddin and then on to the Panjshir Valley, are packed and ready to leave Faizabad, this time by helicopter. It is another old, beat-up machine, parked in a field on the edge of town. A line of spectators, including many children, are waiting for entertainment, some of which I will inadvertently provide. Nasrine wants to devise a way to get me into the helicopter, which like the other lacks steps. Having spied a long board on the field, she oversees a makeshift seesaw, upon which I am to stand, and rise up to the helicopter door. The spectators all draw close, and everyone holds their breath as a member of the Northern Alliance presses one end of the board slowly. I try to stay balanced. I spread my arms out to steady myself. I wobble, regain my balance, and wobble more dangerously. And then I fall off the board and hit the ground.

I am laughing as hard as our audience. Again, I am unceremoniously lifted and pushed into the rusty old helicopter crowded with mujahidin, who are shaking with laughter at me. The helicopter rises and we swoop off for Khoja Bahauddin. I feel a little sad at the thought that I will soon be leaving Afghanistan, but also quite relieved that I am on my way home.

Chapter 6
The Assassins

The helicopter drifts down onto the same green field where we first landed. The Amu Dar'ya River still flows on one side, amber cliffs still loom on the other, and the jeep, filled with young men from the foreign ministry, again brakes with a swirl of dust beside us. We are back in Khoja Bahauddin, and it feels almost like coming home.

Yet I quickly sense a palpable difference. Certainly I have changed; no longer fit and eager, I am tired and ready to go home. But in addition, the young ministry men there to meet the helicopter are no longer smiling and immaculate. They seem exhausted. Our reception is different as well: when we first flew in, the vans took us directly to the front section of the compound, and we were given our lovely suite in the new guest-house villa. This time we are driven to the back half of the compound and all our bags are piled up in one of the small rooms in the old building. The atmosphere in the compound is now perceptibly charged with uneasiness. There are still other guests, but they are no longer gathered informally, convivially. Anxiety pollutes and hangs in the air.

We quickly learn the reason for the change. Nasrine brings news that the Taliban have gone on the offensive. All through the summer there has been a buildup of Taliban and Al Qaeda fighters. As many as sixteen thousand are now massed along the edge of the Shomali Plains, a once-fertile area that has become a no-man's-land bordering Massoud's front line. Among the opposition's troops are many Arabs, Pakistanis, Uzbeks, and Muslim ethnic minorities from China. On the previous Tuesday, there was a battle on the road to Kabul. Prisoners were taken and several hundred men on both sides were killed or wounded. Nasrine is quickly told that all of us, Sara, Mary, Nasrine, and I, will leave for the Panjshir Valley that afternoon. We do not yet know that all foreign visitors are being evacuated from the compound.

I have a great desire to go to the famous Panjshir Valley, reputed to be exceptionally beautiful, surrounded by the towering peaks of the Hindu Kush. It is a traditional visit for all admirers of Massoud, an opportunity to visit his homeland and the base from which he launched his legendary rebuffs of Soviet attacks. But I cannot extend my stay further, and I am tired.

Up to now, I haven't considered exactly how I will get back to Tajikistan. But with Nasrine and the others getting ready to leave, I have to clarify my plans. I consider my options, but the facts never change: first, I need a Northern Alliance helicopter to take me to the Tajik airfield at Kulab; second, I need a car for the long drive from Kulab to Dushanbe; third, there is only one plane a week that goes from Dushanbe to Germany; and fourth, the next plane leaves in three days.

In order to be on the plane to Munich on September 11, I need to be in Dushanbe on the tenth to take care of my visa and ticket. So I must travel from Khoja Bahauddin to Dushanbe on the ninth—tomorrow.

Then I ponder the imponderables: will a helicopter be available to get me out of the country? The ministry men are already strained, coping with visitors while preparing for the possibility of battle. Further, I will need a translator to arrange transport from Kulab to Dushanbe.

I find myself becoming frightened. The drone of helicopters

flying over the compound reassures me somewhat that an aircraft may be available. I have no way of knowing that the helicopters are only transporting foreigners to Panjshir. Nasrine has dragooned a car and whisked Sara off to town to telephone her employer in California yet again to get her agreement for Sara to go with them to Panjshir. But Nasrine is my only means of negotiating this country. Will she really take off and leave me alone in Khoja Bahauddin, the only woman among all the tired, anxious, Dari-speaking young men on Assim's staff? I find it hard to believe that she is not worried about me. For the first time I feel not just old, but frail, unable to cope. I know that without medication my arthritis will become painful and my spinal stenosis will make my legs incredibly weak; I know that I will not be able to negotiate difficult terrain if much walking is required. Without speaking the language, I will not be able to even communicate with anyone. I decide to confide my fears to Mary.

She is in one of the guest rooms, sitting cross-legged on the floor with four men, teaching them a card game that she had picked up from her grandchildren on her last visit to the United States. She seems totally relaxed. Perhaps she has absorbed the philosophy of *inshallah*—translated roughly, "if God wills it"—the ubiquitous term in many Muslim countries for letting go of things outside one's control. Jaheen is learning the card game, as is Fahim Dashti, a young photojournalist who has been studying in Paris with Reporters Without Borders and who has known Massoud since childhood. Mary quickly ends the game and joins me when she sees how worried I look. I explain my dilemma and confess my feelings of abandonment. Mary sympathizes and agrees that she and Sara can and should go on alone and Nasrine should remain with me.

When Nasrine returns, I take her aside. "Nasrine. What about me? What will happen if you go off to Panjshir this afternoon? I don't feel comfortable with no one here who speaks English."

"You'll be fine, Barbara. Assim will take care of you and see that you get to Tajikistan."

"But Nasrine," I burst out, "you can't just go off and leave me! What if there are no helicopters available! Assim is much too busy with everything else. I can't be a burden on him. And what happens in Kulab? How will I get to Dushanbe?" I am very angry. "Nasrine, you can't just go off."

"Barbara, you're being difficult," she retorts, growing angry in turn. "You're making it hard on everyone. They've asked us to leave this afternoon. If I stay behind, that means that Mary and Sara must stay behind too."

Mary, who has come over to us, says, "Nasrine, I have traveled throughout Afghanistan for twenty-five years. I don't need you to take care of us. Sara and I will go on today as they want us to."

Nasrine's first response is always impulsive and negative, but she is ultimately reasonable. She acknowledges that it is not safe to leave me and soon enough comes to terms with our joint dilemma. A short time later, Mary and Sara clamber into one of the trucks that pulls into the compound. Forlornly I hug Mary, knowing I may never see her again. Nasrine and I wave as they leave with all the other foreigners.

The compound feels strange, so empty and quiet. Then Assim calls us into his office and gives me the bad news. I will not be able to leave the next day. Tajikistan's borders are still closed for its tenth anniversary of independence and will not open again until the eleventh. Even if a helicopter were available to take me across the border on the eleventh, there is no way to get to Dushanbe in time to make the plane to Munich; nor would I have time to arrange my visas. There is no other choice: I will have to stay another week. Both Nasrine and I are hard hit by this latest setback. Assim tries hard to reassure me that it is still possible for some sort of arrangements to be made that will get me to Dushanbe.

Nasrine and I gloomily go to our denuded room, emptied of

all luggage except our own bags beside the one high double bed. We sit on the bed and go over all that has to be done—another call to her husband asking him to change my ticket once again; a call to friends in Munich who expect to meet me; a call to my family. As dusk falls and it gets cooler, we go outside. Jaheen, not part of the ministry staff and with no work to do, joins us, and we sink into the plastic chairs on the outside concrete corridor. We sit in silence, each wrapped in his or her own thoughts, and watch stars begin to spot the softly darkening sky. It is very tranquil, but I cannot relax, cannot absorb or be comforted by the warmth of the evening. I am beset by apprehension.

Another foreigner has been left behind, a withdrawn and haggard-looking Frenchman, Roland—we never learn his last name—whom we see the next morning. He is a member of a French aid organization and has been waiting for two months for an interview with Massoud. He sits silently as far as possible from us, avoiding any eye contact. He makes me increasingly uncomfortable. I find him eerie and I suggest to Nasrine that he is either mentally ill or an opium addict, and I am worried about our safety. She thinks Roland is all right, probably depressed from the heat and from having hung around for so long. Our door has a key, and also, she points out, several of the men always sleep outside on the ground, not far from the room, so we hardly have to worry.

At the time I do not know that two other foreigners, the Arab journalists who accompanied us to the near by refugee camp, have also been allowed to stay. They sleep and eat in their room and stay there in the heat of day as well as the cool of dawn or evening. They arrived at Khoja Bahauddin before us, in the same helicopter as Shoukria.

That night, I use the big bed, piled high as usual with dirty mattresses. I unroll my sleeping bag and, without bothering to unpack, lie down. Nasrine unrolls her pad and beds down on the floor. Hardly a breeze comes in. Neither of us can sleep.

Then I hear Nasrine whisper, "Barbara, I've been thinking.

I don't think the compound was evacuated just because it's vulnerable to a Taliban attack. I think it's possible that Massoud is staying next door, in the villa."

"Really?" I whisper. My heart begins to beat more rapidly.

"If that's so," Nasrine sounds thrilled, "maybe we can get to interview him after all." She is now not so unhappy about having to stay with me.

I wake up early Sunday morning, September 9, step over Nasrine, unlock our door, and go out. Jaheen and some of the other young men are asleep on thin pads unrolled on the gravel. I walk over to the latrine as quietly as I can in the heavy walking boots I habitually wear outside town. When I push open the crude wooden door, I reel back from the odor, worse than usual. But I use the latrine, there being no alternative. Back outside, in the fresh morning air, I long to walk down to the river, but a foreign woman alone and dressed in a sleeveless shirt would, I know, be impolitic. A helicopter roars overhead; I hope it isn't taking Massoud away, if indeed he is in the villa.

Around noon, Nasrine and I get a ride into town to use the satellite phone. I also want to buy a traditional Afghan shirt, the kameez, so that the long sleeves will keep flies off my arms. Zubair is again our driver and tells us that they have had thirty groups of guests just in the short time since our last stay.

In the dusty town square, the jeep pulls up in front of a shop, and Zubair waits in the car while Nasrine and I go in to call her husband. Then she explains to the shopkeeper that I want a kameez and he goes next door to have a tailor finish one off for me. While we wait for the neckband to be sewn on, the shopkeeper and Nasrine sit on the floor and converse. He tells her that he had a much better shop in Taloqan, but left after the Taliban took over the town. Now he competes with many other little one-room shops like his.

Suddenly, we hear a grinding of gears as Zubair guns the jeep and roars off. We are stunned. Why has he left us? Shortly after, a man comes to the door of the shop and whispers to the owner. Nasrine thinks she catches the word "Massoud," but cannot get the rest. The shopkeeper comes back, sits down beside Nasrine, a lost, somber expression on his face. Nasrine and I stare at each other. The shopkeeper, almost speaking to himself, grimly says, in Dari, "Massoud should have five lives. If Massoud is killed, we are all dead."

Nasrine translates the shopkeeper's words and I feel a shiver run down my spine. We are both worried that Zubair has not returned. I restlessly wander over to the door and see smoke billowing from the direction of the compound. I do not say anything because once before when I had worried about smoke and told the others, it turned out to be from a brick factory. My kameez is brought in. The shopkeeper gets up, then says he has to leave. We follow and he closes the shop, locks the door, and walks off. The square is totally empty. Wind swirls the dust. Suddenly a dilapidated car pulls up, and the driver leans out and speaks to Nasrine, who pulls me into the vehicle. "Don't panic," she says, "but it looks like there has been an explosion at the compound." She looks more panicked than I feel, but we both become increasingly tense as the hunched driver jams down on the accelerator, forcing the car to careen over the rocky, deserted road.

There is a great silence. The sun burns down; it seems as though we are driving through a lifeless zone. The normally bustling road in front of the compound is empty. The farm women who drive their cattle to the river below, the children who sit astride animals laden with water cans, the construction workers across the bluff—all have vanished. At the open gate we jump out of the car. Then, we stand rigid with shock and horror.

The stink of doused fire fills my lungs and makes my stomach heave. Over the wall that divides the compound, we can see the villa. Smoke has blackened its walls, and its windows have been blown out. Black cinders float in the air and drift down onto our heads. Jaheen and the other young men walk back and forth aimlessly, in a daze. Roland is slumped even deeper than usual in one of the chairs.

Slowly, disjointedly, we learn what has happened.

The two Arab journalists staying at the guesthouse were taken to the villa by Assim and Dashti. As Nasrine surmised, Massoud had indeed been staying there, with his comrade Massoud Khalili, the Afghan ambassador to India. Before taking off on a reconnaissance flight, Massoud had finally agreed to be interviewed. They all assembled in the villa's reception room. The Arabs began the interview with questions about bin Laden, which made the Afghans uneasy. Then one of the Arabs focused his camera on Massoud and, as he clicked the shutter, the camera fired a bullet at Massoud. The other Arab leaned over and detonated explosives packed in his belt. He was blown apart, and most of the others in the room were severely burned in the blazing explosion except for the other assassin who ran out of the house. Bewildered guards rushed in the direction of the villa, while he ran right past them and out of the compound. A few guards pulled themselves together and gave chase. They caught the man and locked him in one of the compound rooms, identical to ours; but, dazed by the day's events, they left him unguarded and he got away again, jumping out the back window into the open field and fleeing down to the river.

Zubair had received the news on his cell phone, which was why he left us stranded in town while he raced back to the compound. As he drove up, he saw the assassin running toward the river. He joined in the chase, shouting, "Capture him, capture him, don't shoot. Don't kill him. We have to interrogate the devil." The Arab, at the edge of the river, turned to face the guards and one of them fired and killed him.

The shopkeeper's dire prophesy, "If Massoud is killed, we are all dead!" echoes in my head as Nasrine and I ask over and over, "Was Massoud killed? Was Massoud wounded? How is Assim? Where are they?"

Jaheen, white-faced, keeps repeating in a choking voice,

"No one was killed. They will all be all right." Finally he breaks down sobbing and admits that Assim was killed instantly when he threw himself in front of Massoud as the bomb was set off. The terrorists' attempt to assassinate the legendary Amer Saheb—"Dear Boss"—is too shocking, too catastrophic, for me to absorb, or even cry over; even when I finally comprehend the fact that Assim, a human being I have known and tremendously admired, has been murdered, I am devastated but still cannot cry. I am locked into a state from which there is no easy relief.

As the rest of the garbled story slowly emerges, Nasrine and I listen with growing disbelief. While Massoud was flown out by helicopter, the wounded men in the villa were carried to cars and driven to a nearby hospital. But, horror heaped on horror, in the confusion, Assim was left behind. Only when the hospital reported him missing did they go back to find his body still in the burning embers. Zubair is now tending the body and has taken charge of the compound.

Nasrine and I sit, we stand, we walk around. Our grief is subsumed by rage. We are furious with everyone. "What kind of stupidity," we ask each other incredulously, "can have possessed their security to allow terrorists to walk into a meeting with Massoud with explosives in their belt?"

All afternoon, Nasrine intercepts everyone who walks over from the other side. She asks each one if she can be taken to the villa to photograph the dead assassin. She says that she can get his picture to our FBI or CIA for tracing. She pleads with them. But security has been taken over by an elite group of soldiers, unlike any I have seen in Afghanistan before, even in photographs. These men are more in the image of American Special Forces. They wear high, lace-up boots and camouflage uniforms, quite unlike the typical mujahidin in his baggy uniform, part kameez and part army, always topped with the soft felt pakol hat that is the traditional head covering in the region. The grim-faced troops shake off questions, ignore us as irrelevant. They stride back and forth between the two sections of the compound. I find out later that they are part of Massoud's regular troops and had come with him to the villa. Our compound is not a military base, but part of the foreign ministry, and we had never seen Massoud's military base, called the Garden, which is not far from the compound.

Around four o'clock, Zubair and the other young men of Assim's staff, his comrades, carry a rough wooden coffin, still open, into our part of the compound. It holds Assim's body, bathed and bound in burial wrappings. They fetch a bed frame from one of the rooms and put the coffin on it so that it will not rest on the dirt. They scrounge through the emptied rooms, searching for a cloth large enough to cover the coffin to keep away the dust and insects. It is brutally hot. An electric fan from the villa is put on a table at the head of the coffin, a line of electric extension cords is rigged together, the generator is turned on, and the fan slowly stirs the scorching air to protect Assim's body from the last heat of the day.

Men begin to arrive, gathering to pray. Zubair, gently, apologetically tells us that they are expecting many guests for the all-night vigil of Koran recitations and that we and Roland will have to leave. We are driven a few miles away to an enclosed group of buildings, and Nasrine and I are led into a small one-room mud-brick and woven-reed hut.

We sit on opposite sides of the room, on thin pallets on the dirt floor. From two small slits of windows, too high on the wall to see out of, the red glow from the setting sun fades until the room is only dimly lit by a kerosene lamp on the floor. We are exhausted, too drained to speak. I lie down on the hard floor. I feel as though my bones will break. Nasrine sits up and smokes one cigarette after another.

The owner of this house, a burly, bearded man, comes in with a young servant, whom he brusquely instructs to bring us supper. The frail boy brings in a basin of water for us to wash our hands before we eat. He returns, his arms quivering under the weight of a large tray of food.

The owner's manner changes when he speaks to Nasrine.

To her he is warm and sociable, pointing out the amenities, which include a latrine just outside our door. We must not be frightened, he tells us, the servant boy will sleep outside our door and be on call to serve our needs. Nasrine and our host sit cross-legged and eat. I sit up to drink some tea but I cannot eat. I lie down again and shift my body awkwardly on the hard ground, then roll over and groan, hoping to sleep but instead listening to the drone of unintelligible voices as Nasrine and the man eat and converse in Dari. I glimpse Zubair coming in to inquire about us, but I just lie there, trying to fit my arthritic body into the hollows of the dirt floor.

When the man leaves I push myself up. It takes all of my strength. "Nasrine," I say, "please take my picture."

"Later, later," she says impatiently.

Awkwardly, painfully, I get to my feet and totter over to her with the camera. "Please, Nasrine, take my picture."

Back on my pallet, I slump exhausted against the wall. The flash brightens the room momentarily. I sink back down.

Nasrine tells me that it was the worst night of her life. She was terrified that the assassination was just the begining, that the Taliban was on the threshold of attack. She was too afraid to sleep. I guess I was too numb to be afraid and fell into a deep sleep, blanking out mind and body.

The next morning Nasrine recounts her long conversation with our host, who told her Assim had been "like a brother" to him for some fifteen years. Assim, he said, had been born in Kabul to a Panjshir family and studied economics at the university. After graduation, he founded a mixed-gender "cultural center" for computer studies, which, according to his friend, had over a thousand students and fifty-four teachers, some of whom were women. Assim's wife was a Kabul high school graduate; in traditional fashion, they were cousins on his mother's side. When Kabul fell to the Taliban, Assim and his wife moved to Panjshir where he worked as a translator. Later, he joined the mujahidin government's Foreign Ministry and moved to Taliqon. Our host worried about Assim's wife, repeating what we had heard earlier, that she was not well, and that she and their three young children live in Dushanbe, where she is receiving medical care.

During the years in Taloqan, Assim helped organize a working women's political group, a project he loved. We had met three of those women in Faizabad when they visited Nasrine in my room. Assim also worked with human rights groups. When the Taliban captured Taloqan, he was sent to Khoja Bahauddin to build the compound that would serve as a base for Massoud and a guesthouse for the ministry.

Assim had once told Nasrine that he had moved five times since the Taliban overran Kabul. "I sometimes find it hard to get up and get clean and start the day," he admitted to her. "I've given up caring about my surroundings." But he did get up each day and, as director of the compound, took care of all the visitors, the journalists, the aid workers, mullahs, the commanders, everyone who could contribute to the demise of the Taliban.

Although few Afghan men whom I met were feminists, Assim appeared to be one. "The work I most care about is with the women," he told Nasrine. "They must be there to rebuild Afghanistan when we recover our country." Shoukria had helped arrange our stay with the Northern Alliance, thanks to her friendship with Assim. They had met when Shoukria first began to organize among the women in areas occupied by the Taliban and in internal-refugee camps, after the Taliban overran the Shomali Plain, just north of Kabul, in the summer of 1999. The Taliban militia had killed civilians, torched their homes, machine-gunned their livestock, destroyed fields of crops, and blasted irrigation canals. Thousands of fruit trees—mulberry, apple, walnut—were cut down, and vineyards burned. The desperate population fled the Plain. Assim was with Shoukria as she filmed the flight of some fifty to sixty thousand men, women, and children struggling through the narrow Salang tunnel to the Panjshir Valley. I watched that film in Nasrine's house, what seems eons ago.

Assim spent his last night in the one-room hut where we now are, talking with our host into the late hours. According to his friend, Assim said he did not like "the smell" of the Arab journalists. Assim always wanted to be "of service to the people," his friend said. "He had a soft heart."

At about 10:30 one of the ministry men comes and takes us back to the Northern Alliance compound. I climb in and out of the jeep with difficulty; I seem to have aged overnight and feel suspended in time. Roland has been brought back also. He, Nasrine, and I are the only guests. The sun beats down relentlessly and becomes part of the burden of sadness with which the entire community is consumed. One day passes into the next without news about my leaving. Our meals are minimal—rice, nan, tea, an occasional vegetable. We have neither heart nor energy to undertake much personal care. Dipping into the container of polluted river water in the "bath" room next to the latrine to wipe the encrusted sand off my face and arms seems almost pointless. Nasrine and I are so overcome by the horror of the assassination plot and by the unyielding heat that we spend many hours stretched out in a stupor, me on the bed, she on the floor mat. Nasrine digs out a new book on Afghanistan for me and gives me photocopies of political analyses. There is nothing else to read.

Nasrine, at least, is able to spend a lot of time with Zubair. She meets other men who come to the compound and in the evening joins the staff as they start the generator and listen to international news. She urges me to go to Zubair and plead for him to contact someone to get me a helicopter. But I hesitate, knowing how desolate he feels at the death of his beloved friend Assim. As the days stretch on, the sound of a helicopter flying overhead is like a jolt of electricity, but they always pass by and disappear.

Each time we ask about Massoud, we are told that he is alive, seriously burned but alive. Actually, we later learn that Massoud was immediately killed, along with Assim. Massoud's body had been flown to a hospital in Tajikistan and General Mohammed Qasim Fahim, the second in command of Massoud's military forces, arrived soon after. He, along with other Northern Alliance officials, agreed that the death should be kept secret for the time being. So the troops knew only that their commander was badly wounded.

The assassins were Tunisian, identified by photographs that Shoukria's journalist friend, Francoise Causse, had taken earlier. They had entered Afghanistan via Pakistan, traveling with stolen Belgian passports and with visas forged by an Arab group in Belgium that provided many forged travel documents for young militants going to Al Qaeda training camps.

One day, in desperation, I do go in to see Zubair. Nasrine and I have agreed that I should lay on a heavy "poor sick old woman" act, which is not far from the truth. As I tell him how desperate I feel, how my medication is almost gone, my tears begin to flow uncontrollably—as it turns out, no acting is necessary. I sense his deep sympathy and feel even more inconsolable and lost in the mire of Afghanistan's troubles. I know he has no control over the allocation of available helicopters. I tell Zubair how great is my sorrow over Assim's death and his eyes fill with tears. He excuses himself and I watch him outside, head bent, shoulders shaking. I cannot continue to complain when I know the desperation of these men. So many of them have been kind and gracious to me, treating me like a grandmother. Most have not seen their own grandmothers—or mothers, or wives, or children—for years.

Nasrine and I go over and over different scenarios for my departure. Of course, our original plan assumed that we would fly from Dushanbe directly into Afghanistan, that I would spend a week there and return by plane to Dushanbe while Nasrine and Sara spent another week or two in Panjshir. How innocent we were! Now we need to know the name of the Afghan official in Kalab who can arrange transportation. We need to know who I should contact in Dushanbe to translate and to help with potential ticket or visa problems. We don't have many answers. One afternoon a man named Habidulah Allahyar comes to see me. He is stationed in Nimroz, an Iranian border town. With Nasrine translating, he assures me that the Afghan Embassy knows about me and they are trying to get me out, but that Tajikistan's border remains closed. He does not explain why he has come and I wonder if, for some reason, they are thinking of getting me out through Iran. I am incredibly appreciative that there are people concerned about me.

I intend to leave my sleeping bag and other superfluous items behind, so I repack, distributing my money inside different pockets, assuming that I will still go via the Tajik airfield and may have to face the customs officials there. Time drags on.

"Barbara," Nasrine murmurs to me one day as we lay spread out on the beds, rendered half unconscious by the heat. "I am so happy that you were the one to take this trip with me."

I look over at her. "What do you mean, Nasrine?"

"You have coped so well. Oh, my God, the tragedy, the horror! If someone else had come, she might have become hysterical. Or a group! How could I have taken care of a bunch of hysterical, wailing women?"

I laugh. "Wouldn't it have been horrible if we had been successful and had brought a big delegation of unknown women?"

But the waiting, the uncertainty of when and how we will be able to leave, is wearing us both down. Although only four days have passed, each hour stretches endlessly and I feel suffocated within an impermeable curtain of time. My constant concern is how to apportion the few remaining precious pain and anti-inflammatory tablets. Without medication, I fear the weakness of my legs if we have to leave on foot. I do not want to panic so I clamp down hard on my imagination and refuse to speculate.

And then, on the morning of September 13, the call comes. We have performed our perfunctory ablutions and have had our tea and nan on the floor in our room, carried in by the sweet porter. Nasrine has gone out and I am fussing around with my bag when I hear their cries: "Barbara, Barbara, Come quick! Come quick!" All the men in the compound are shouting, copying the English words from Nasrine.

She bursts into the room, shouting "Barbara, a helicopter is here! Hurry, grab your bag. There isn't much time. They are waiting for you right now. But you must hurry!"

She zips up my largest bag. I am panic-stricken. I struggle to tie my clumsy boots. "My passport!" I cry. "My passport is in the suitcase you're closing," I yell to Nasrine.

Hysterically, we push through the garments in the bag, looking for the passport. "I've got it!" I yell, and Nasrine zips the bag and runs with it. I grab everything else and, stumbling over my half-tied boots, run out of the room. All the guys are jumping up and down. Zubair is gunning the jeep so hard that I am terrified it will stall.

Nasrine and I jump in, someone throws my bags in the jeep, and I lean out to kiss Jaheen goodbye as the car shoots out the gate and up the road, and then rocks and sways as we pull onto the pitted dirt path that winds down to the riverside field. I gasp when I see the huge, gleaming military helicopter resting on the field. Tall, uniformed, armed men stand talking in small groups. Another figure in black civilian clothes stands alone, with his back to us. When Nasrine recognizes the man, she pulls back into the car, painfully aware of her disheveled appearance. Zubair grabs my bags and pushes me ahead, rushing us to the helicopter and shoving me onto the steps at its door. I turn around; I want to thank him, to kiss him three times in the Afghan way, to hug him good-bye, but he has already turned and is walking back to the jeep.

I step into the enormous body of the helicopter and sit down on one of the padded benches lining the sides. The soldiers quickly climb in; obviously they delayed their departure for me. An armchair covered by an oriental carpet is near the entrance.

As soon as the civilian man climbs in and sits down in the armchair, the helicopter blades begin to turn, and the aircraft swiftly lifts and soars over the gleaming river. I recognize the man in the armchair as Dr. Abdullah Abdullah, Massoud's close friend and Afghanistan's foreign minister. During the hour's flight he never glances my way, never smiles. His shadowed face is grim.

A familiar-looking man is next to me and leans over to ask me a question, but the roaring noise of the helicopter fills the interior and I have difficulty hearing him. Finally, it dawns on me that this is Massoud's nephew, the defense attaché at the Afghan embassy in Dushanbe. He is asking me about Sara. I explain that she is in the Panjshir Valley to film Mary, but that is as much conversation as I can manage.

The trip is taking much longer than before. I wonder where we are headed, but suddenly I can no longer think as an overwhelming happiness swells and surges, abates, and then surges again through my body. I have survived and I am going home! Absurdities burst in my brain: I will soon bathe my whole body, wash my hair, and stand under hot water. I am going to sleep under clean sheets, drink coffee, and have a glass of liquor. I want steak and salad. Abruptly, my brain switches. I seem to have no volition over my emotions or thoughts. I think of the others left behind, of the murdered Assim; despairing Jaheen; and Zubair, always ready to help. Tears fill my eyes at Zubair's kindness to me—a stranger and a foreigner, who has so much while he has so little. Zubair must have pleaded with his chief, Dr. Abdullah, to delay his schedule and allow me on his plane. I feel no one has ever done so much for me. I am filled with distress that I have not been able to thank him.

The helicopter lands at a remote section of a major airport. The military men disembark first, then Dr. Abdullah and Massoud's nephew. No one looks in my direction. I search for my bags. There is no one to help me. I pull my two bags over to the door and hurry down the steps. I call out for help but there is no one. I see the minister and his entourage striding away. Panic and adrenaline give me strength and I tug the bags down, pull up the handle of my wheeled suitcase and run after the men, dragging the bags behind me.

The group of men grows smaller as they recede into the distance down the long runway. Even in my panic, some particle of my mind is infinitely amused at the vision of this old woman running and stumbling, pulling her bags and desperately yelling, "Wait, wait, please wait for me!" Then the group is gone. Large black cars and vans pull off the runway.

I stop running and slowly walk on, not sure where I am and what I should do. Still far from any airport building, I come to a small white car. Two men get out, take my bags, open the back door of the automobile and motion to me to get in. They are smiling and one says in English, "Did you think we would leave you?" The Afghan Foreign Ministry has sent a car for me.

I gratefully sink back in the seat. I don't know where I am or what will happen next, and for the moment, I don't especially care. What will happen will happen. Inshallah. We drive out of the airport onto a side road—no queuing up for passport scrutiny, no bureaucracy, no customs. I envision myself stumbling down the runway just minutes before and feel as though I have become part of a Keystone Kops routine. But I cannot stop thinking about the tragedy I have left behind.

When we leave the airport, I realize I am in Dushanbe. The city seems impossibly ravishing as I look out of the car window at rows of lofty green trees; wide, clean boulevards; people striding briskly on paved sidewalks; new automobiles, trams, and buses; functioning traffic lights; and police. I am back in what is to me normal life. No burqas, not even many headscarves. I watch the women on the sidewalks, some in Western dress, others in their colorful national garment, hair free, faces bare.

The car pulls into the circular driveway of a hotel that seems incredibly glamorous after Khoja Bahauddin. The Afghans hand me my bags, smile, bow, and are gone. I carry my suitcases up a few wide marble steps into the lobby, suddenly a little panicky at being on my own. I press my travel purse to my side, passport and credit card safe inside. I will be all right. The lobby is empty. The women at the registration counter look puzzled by my unexpected appearance—there are few single foreign women wandering around Dushanbe. They call over another woman who speaks a little English; she takes my passport and asks me to wait a few minutes. Suddenly very tired, and feeling downright dirty, I gingerly sit down on a sofa and look up at a small television screen hung from a ceiling rafter. I see a news report of a skyscraper tower collapsing, fires bursting from buildings, explosions. I cannot understand the language; it might be Russian.

A tall man stands nearby, also watching the TV. "Do you speak English?" I ask. He nods.

"Do you know what country that is?" He looks at me strangely. "You don't know?" he asks, with what sounds like a French accent. He bends down to me, then slowly says, "That's New York."

"But, but . . . what?" I stammer.

"Terrorists flew planes into the World Trade Center in New York. There are many dead." I feel a blow, as though I have been punched, hard.

A French Afghan woman joins us, a journalist traveling with the man I have been speaking to, who is also a journalist. I tell her where I have been and why. Her name is Nilab and she knows Nasrine and Shoukria. She rapidly brings me up to date on the attacks in New York and Washington, D.C., and tells me that there are no flights to the United States.

I am too stunned to fully understand. I had just begun to gain a sense of normalcy that instantly drains away. I accept a key and follow a porter, who takes my bag and leads me to my room. I strip and walk into the bathroom, turn the hot water on in the shower, step in, and stand under the steaming water. I just stand there under the hot water without feeling. I soap my body, slowly and carefully, over every bit of skin, pour shampoo

on my head and scrub and scrub. After a while I step out and
rub myself down with a bath towel. I pull back the bedcover, lie
down naked on the starched white sheets of the bed, and then
my body starts to convulse. Great sobs move up from my stomach, through my body and come out my mouth in loud gasping
groans. I shake and sob and after a while tears start to flow.
    This goes on for a long while, but then my body finally stops
reacting, my mind takes over. I need to know what has happened. I see a TV and turn it on, switching channels until I
come to an English-language news station. I lie down again,
pull the covers up, and over and over again watch pictures of the
attacks, now two days old but still playing continuously on the
TV.
    It is late afternoon. I open my suitcase, put on clean clothes,
and go downstairs for some food and then go back to the room,
lie down, turn on the BBC, and keep it on all night as I sleep,
wake, cry, and fall asleep again.
    The next morning, I go over what I have to do before the
plane to Munich leaves in several days. First I call Khosrow, our
translator when we first arrived in Dushanbe en route to Afghanistan. He will come to the hotel that morning. Then I call family and friends in the States and in Munich and leave messages
on their answering machines. I need to know if everyone is OK
and to let them know I am all right. My instinctive first stop, in
a situation like this, would be the American embassy, but Nasrine has told me the United States has no embassy in Dushanbe.
Before Khosrow arrives I call the number of a Tajik woman who
speaks English, given to me by Connie Borde from French
NEGAR. The woman will meet me that evening.
    Shoukria, who had left Faizabad for Dushanbe, is still in
there and she comes to the hotel with Khosrow. After embracing and weeping together, we spend some time attempting to
analyze the meaning and consequences of the attacks in the
United States. With her slight command of English and my
even poorer French, communication is frustrating for both of

us. I am able to make Shoukria understand that in Khoja Bahauddin we had not known about the 9/11 attacks. She is puzzled, as she knows that people in Kabul are aware of what has happened, and that there were radios at the compound. Later I learn that Nasrine, Zubair, and the compound staff heard BBC reports about the attacks on the satellite radio. Nasrine wanted me to know, but those gentle young Afghans insisted I not be told; they did not want me to worry about my Washington family, knowing there was no way for me to contact them.

Talking with Shoukria, I begin to realize what the 9/11 attacks may mean for the people of Afghanistan, since their country is the home base of Al Qaeda and its Taliban supporters. Shoukria has helped the Afghan community in Dushanbe compose a statement to the United Nations, as intermediary to the United States, asking that Kabul not be bombed in any act of retribution. All the refugees, including Shoukria, have family in the capital.

Khosrow arrives and we go to the airport, where we track down a clerk, who locates my reservation on her computer. It seems like a miracle. I have a ticket and will leave in a few days.

When I get back to the hotel, the lobby is filled with newly arrived journalists rushing back and forth, encumbered by multiple cameras, bulging briefcases, and cell phones. They bring with them an atmosphere of excitement, an enviable sense of being in the know and of collegiality. Male and female, from many different countries, they rush in, crouch over drinks, talk excitedly, rush off. Rumors proliferate—borders are closed, no civil planes allowed to leave; the United States is preparing for war and revenge. Someone says that the United States will use Dushanbe's airport as a base to launch attacks on Afghanistan and that there will be no civilian flights in the foreseeable future. I go out to dinner with Connie Borde's friend, Zarona, who tells me that the US embassy has moved to Almaty, Kazakhstan, but that a small Tajik crew provides a few services for the embassy. Zarona calls there and leaves a message with my name and hotel. She tells me that there was a taped State Department travel warning for US citizens in Dushanbe, advising them to avoid crowds and remain inside after dark.

Khosrow comes the next day with news that Nasrine's husband, Max, and her brother, Omar, have called and want Nasrine to get out of Afghanistan. I begin to feel anxious about my own situation. I call my sister to get a chain of my friends to call the State Department and insist they help me to leave.

My sister calls back to report that the State Department will get me out via Moscow and to expect someone from the embassy that day. He arrives soon after and introduces himself as the regional security officer. He seems annoyed at having to come from Almaty to meet me and proceeds to interview me in an officious—and suspicious—manner. Having expected a warm fellow American on a rescue mission, I am offended to be treated as if I am being interrogated by the CIA.

"What were you doing in Afghanistan?" he demands.

"I was on a mission to observe the condition of women."

Raised eyebrow. "What organization are you traveling with?"

"I am traveling as an individual but I have been with an Afghan American friend and we both work with an Afghan women's organization called NEGAR."

"Is that a United Nations NGO?"

"I don't believe so."

"Where did you go in Afghanistan?"

"I was in Khoja Bahauddin and Faizabad."

"Who arranged your trip?" And so it goes. I grant that after 9/11 he has a reason to be suspicious of anyone coming out of Afghanistan. But it is unpleasant.

He tells me to be ready at 6:00 the next morning, when I will be picked up by an embassy clerk and taken to the airport. I tell him that I had planned to go with a British friend I have met in the hotel, in her staff car. He coldly brushes me off. "Mrs. Bick, you either go in the embassy car or we will not accept any responsibility for getting you out of Tajikistan. If we are responsible for you, and there is any delay in the scheduled flight tomorrow, our driver will arrange for you to be put on a plane for Almaty and from there to Moscow." I decide to go along with anything he asks.

That night, bags packed and in bed, I realize how I have cut off thinking about Afghanistan, about the aftermath of Massoud's murder and the pain of Assim's death, and about what the future may bring. I still cannot bear to think about what our response will be to the attacks in the United States. I know in my heart of hearts that having survived this experience through the great kindness of so many Afghans, I must somehow be of service to them in the future.

I hardly sleep. At 6:00 a.m. I get into the large black car beside a Tajik embassy clerk and, as we drive through the silent streets, I am filled with fear for Afghanistan and the people I have met during this incredible voyage.

Two days later I have made it all the way to the States, after spending one night in Munich with dear friends Gisela and Eberhardt Köpp. My plan had been to be with my family on Martha's Vineyard, but instead of going to New York, from which I had booked a flight to the Vineyard, the plane is rerouted to Philadelphia, which is ill prepared for the onslaught of diverted traffic. I push through to what I hope is the line of passengers waiting to proceed through newly implemented security procedures before boarding my next flight.

"Excuse me," I say to the young man waiting in the line behind me. "Would you please watch my bag while I go up to find out if I am in the correct line?"

"Oh, no, you don't!" shouts the man. "You take your goddamn bag with you." And he glares at me.

"OK, OK," I stammer, more puzzled than offended. I take my bag and leave the line to get information. Then it slowly dawns on me. Suspicion. Fear. My bag might contain bombs. I am home, but the terrain has shifted yet again.

It takes many hours to get to the Vineyard, as I navigate this new world of security precautions and cancelled travel options. I have to spend the night in Woods Hole but am on next morning's first ferry to Vineyard Haven. The cloudless blue sky, the deep-blue Sound filled with white sails of end-of-summer boaters, seem not of the real world. The real world to me is now poverty, drought, and oppression. I know that the experience of the past few weeks will be embedded in my very being. But now I shut it down.

The ferry is nearing the dock. With joy, I open up my soul to homecoming. I hurry down to the deck to be among the first stepping off onto land and rush to embrace my waiting family.

Chapter 7

Kabul Redux, 2003

On October 7, 2001, a few minutes after 9:00 p.m. Afghanistan time, the US retaliates against the Taliban and Al Qaeda, striking thirty-one military targets and Al Qaeda training camps across the country. It is a modest attack, as such bombing raids go; nonetheless, I am thrown into emotional turmoil. I feel exultant that the women and children, the people of Afghanistan, will be freed from the Taliban nightmare, but I am pained that so many of my friends are actively opposed to what they see as just another American intervention.

I long to be close to people who see the broader peril of what the Taliban has done to the people of Afghanistan. I am in touch with Nasrine, but not as much as I would like, because of the erratic condition of the Afghan telephone and Internet systems. After I left Afghanistan, Nasrine went to the Panjshir Valley and joined thousands of mourners at Massoud's funeral. As the Taliban militias fled Kabul before the onslaught of US air attacks and the city was liberated by the Northern Alliance, Nasrine moved to Kabul. Now, she is aflame with hope for the renewal of her beloved country and continues to garner signatures from hundreds of Afghans for NEGAR's declaration.

I hear from Connie Borde in Paris that she is working very hard with Shoukria, who is commuting between Paris and

Kabul. The American expats and the French women in NEGAR are helping to plan and arrange support for a series of seminars in Afghanistan that will provide information to women about the new constitution being drafted, to enable their participation in the process. The draft is Islamic throughout, but it has important democratic elements. It states, for example, that Afghanistan must abide by all international treaties and conventions it has signed, such as the Universal Declaration of Human Rights and the Convention on the Elimination of All Forms of Discrimination Against Women (CEDAW). It also ensures that women will make up at least 16.5 percent of the membership of the upper legislative house.

I am also in email contact with Mary MacMakin. Mary and Sara had met up with a group of Swiss technicians in Panjshir who were setting up a communications bank for the valley, providing heavy batteries, each of which, according to Mary, had to be carried by two men. When the technicians were finished, Sara left for home with her countrymen. For Mary, there was no such easy egress from the valley. She made a harrowing journey on horseback to Pakistan, clad only in her light cotton clothes as she and her guide rode through snow and icy storms over the mountain passes of the Hindu Kush. Now, Mary, too, has jubilantly returned to Kabul after its liberation from the Taliban and begun the process of relocating all her projects. We agree that in the spring, Mary will stay with me on one of her regular trips to the States to visit family and raise funds for her projects.

These contacts are little enough, but they help, to some extent, to ease my overwhelming need to do something for the people of Afghanistan. In some quixotic way, because my life has been so safe and comfortable, I feel beholden to all the women I have met from 1990 to the present, as well as to all the unknown Afghan women and children who have had to endure so much.

When I returned from Afghanistan, I found myself a local

news item: there was a front-page photo of me with Assim in the *Vineyard Gazette*; standing-room-only audience at our local bookstore, the Bunch of Grapes, interviews in the *Cape Cod Times, Boston Herald, Newark Star Ledger*, and Women's ENews. Other interviews followed on television, and NPR's *All Things Considered*, along with a story in *Washington Jewish Week*, which was reprinted in Jewish newspapers around the country.

Now, I watch the fate of Afghanistan with both hope and fear. The US government is still divided over how to proceed with the local forces on the ground. Gary Schroen, a CIA field officer who set up a post-9/11 base in Afghanistan, would write in his 2005 book, *First In: An Insider's Account of How the CIA Spearheaded the War on Terror in Afghanistan*, "General Mahammed Qasim Fahim and the senior Northern Alliance leadership [recognized] that there were grave reservations within the senior ranks of the US government over allowing the Northern Alliance to capture and occupy Kabul. Years of political dealings with the US government had made it painfully clear to the Northern Alliance that there was a strong anti-Tajik lobby within the ranks of senior US policy-makers." The US State Department is apparently worried about Pakistan's angry response if Massoud's Tajiks are allowed to capture and occupy Kabul. But there are also those, including some in the CIA, who have been in and out of Afghanistan for years, who understand the battlefield realities and had long admired Massoud. Above all, the Northern Alliance—officially the United Front—is determined to take Kabul. The capital is surrounded by territory they furiously fought over and which they now occupy. More important, they are driven by the memory of the lives of their brethren sacrificed during the long, lean years when they stood against the Taliban, Al Qaeda, and their Pakistani supporters.

Following the initial bombing raid, the US-led coalition has maintained massive bombing of strategic sites in Afghanistan. By early November 2001, after fierce ground battles, all the major cities in the north are occupied by the mujahidin forces of the United Front. When the last stronghold, Kundiz, is captured on November 25, Pakistani aircraft rescue several thousand Taliban and Al Qaeda soldiers and their military advisers. Two to three thousand more Taliban and Al Qaeda fighters escape into the South Waziristan province of Pakistan, including, according to reports, both Mullah Omar and bin Laden. But the Taliban is routed! On November 14, the Northern Alliance enters Kabul. I have no doubt that at that moment, the image of their commander, Ahmad Shah Massoud, is in the heart and mind of every one of his Tajik troops.

The international community of donor nations, which did so little to help Afghanistan before 9/11, has now leapt into action, pledging billions for reconstruction. In December, the United Nations initiates a conference in Bonn to plan for postwar Afghanistan. It is expected that the four major post-Taliban political factions will be sending, typically, an all-male cast. Instead, a surprising new script is played out: three women are included in the twenty-eight-member delegation—two in the former king's group, one with the Northern Alliance—along with at least two more women attending as advisers. The Bonn meeting sets up an interim government, agreeing on the US-backed Pashtun, Hamid Karzai, as interim president. Three major ministries go to Northern Alliance Tajiks from Panjshir.

As I closely read the US media, I realize that although Massoud is celebrated as a national hero, there is spreading concern over the concentration of power by the Tajiks. This feeling is especially strong among returning refugees who suffered through the mujahidin civil war, which many blame primarily on Rabbani and Massoud, rather than any of the other mujahidin parties such as Hekmatyar's. Women express bitterness against the Northern Alliance for Rabbani's edicts while president requiring women to return to conservative Islamic traditions, including dress. They also bring up his denial of requests for an Afghan delegation to the 1995 UN World Conference on Women in Beijing. I know Nasrine has never believed that Rabbani supported women's rights, but Mary MacMakin, speaking to me about it in Faizibad, said women were free in their dress and able to work everywhere in Kabul until the Taliban. She blamed Hekmatyar for fomenting Kabul's destruction and the civil war. She did acknowledge that all of the mujahidin parties participated in the final frenzy until, as she told it, Massoud withdrew to save the population. I realize there are two stories, at least, in every historic account and both contain some truth.

What I find truly amazing and hopeful, now, is the rapid emergence of Afghan women from their five years of bondage and centuries of oppression. Just days after the liberation of Kabul, women throng the streets, almost all still covered by the burqa, cautious of the new situation, but thrilled at the sight of items for sale such as books, condoms, and hair dryers, all forbidden by the Taliban. Women and girls are clamoring for schools to open and for new schools to replace those destroyed in the past ten years. Hundreds of young women are registering for classes at Kabul University and thousands are seeking jobs at international relief organizations.

Urban, educated, and professional women, many of whom taught, worked, and organized clandestinely during the Taliban terror, are attending several international conferences, including the UN Development Program/World Bank meeting in Islamabad and the roundtable in Brussels on building women's leadership, sponsored by the UN Development Fund for Women (UNIFEM) and the Belgian government. The Afghan Women's Summit for Democracy, also held in Brussels in December, 2001, is called by a broad array of international institutions and groups to implement the UN Security Council's resolution on women, peace, and security, which calls for women's representation in conflict resolution and in rebuilding war-torn societies. The summit is attended by a large, diverse group of Afghan women from within and outside Afghanistan, along with many international women leaders and speakers. All these meetings are set up to ensure women's participation in shaping the future of Afghanistan.

I am astonished to read that women have taken to the streets in Kabul, Herat, and other cities to demonstrate for jobs and security. Even more strange is to read admiring stories in the *New York Times,* the *Washington Post,* and *Vogue* about one of the women organizing them, Suraya Parlika, whom I had interviewed during my first visit to Kabul in 1990, when she was head of the Afghan Red Crescent. She and her family held high positions during the Parcham regime of the Communist PDPA. Parlika, who was unmarried, remained in Afghanistan during the years of the mujahidin and the Taliban, during which she organized the covert All-Afghan Women's Council, which held classes and provided work under supremely dangerous conditions. Now Parlika, at age fifty-seven, is back in the open, still organizing and demanding education and power for women.

On March 20, 2003, the United States begins its "shock and awe" bombing of Iraq despite months of worldwide antiwar demonstrations that bring unprecedented millions of people into the streets. Following the bombing, American ground forces enter Iraq to begin the long battle to vanquish and occupy the country. For Afghanistan, the consequences of this invasion are especially dire.

Through the spring and summer of 2003, as the United States's political attention and armed forces remain concentrated on Iraq, I follow the news from Afghanistan with an increasing sense of dread. The Taliban is already moving back from its sanctuary in Pakistan into the southern provinces, sowing havoc, murdering foreign aid workers, burning girls' schools, and threatening Afghans who work for the government headed by President Karzai. Hekmatyar, the man my Afghan friends consider one of the most sadistic of the mujahidin, has left Iran to join with the Taliban and is reported to be in command of its terrorist forces around Kabul. Their aim is to disrupt the process of returning Afghanistan to a constitutional government.

By the end of September 2003, a new constitution has been drafted—it took eighteen months—and is being circulated throughout Afghanistan. It is crucial that women participate in the discussion of the constitution and participate in the Loya Jirga, the traditional assembly of Afghan leaders that convenes to elect leaders, enact laws, or confront a crisis. That this ancient instrument will be used to ratify the governing document for a new, more inclusive nation enchants me. It reminds me of the Hegelian idea of change—the dialectic in which a thesis is opposed by its antithesis, and in their synthesis, something entirely new is born. I will witness this process in real life as tradition is opposed by modernity, and something new is formed out of both. I do not know what the synthesis will be, but it should be remarkable.

For NEGAR, events have outpaced their five-year petition strategy. This is their moment, their raison d'être, and Nasrine, Shoukria, and the NEGAR volunteers are working with a powerful sense of urgency to ensure that women are part of the Loya Jirga that will ratify a constitution guaranteeing their right to political participation. NEGAR has moved its base from France to Kabul and a group of Afghan women activists have rallied around it. Under the leadership of Shoukria, Nasrine, and the French NEGAR leader Chantal Veron, and with Connie Borde's Paris-based links to institutional support, local women in provincial towns are learning through a series of three-day conferences how to participate in the constitutional debate. NEGAR will hold its final, large conference in early December, prior to the meeting of the Loya Jirga, bringing these women together in Kabul.

Until our visit in 2001, Nasrine had not been to Afghanistan for thirty-seven years, and now she has hardly left, returning to the States to visit her family for only a few weeks at a time. During her two years in Kabul, in addition to her indefatigable work with NEGAR, Nasrine has become an associate professor at Kabul University, where her father was once president; has established the Roqia Center for Women's Rights, Studies and Development, named after her mother; and has begun a pathbreaking adult literacy program designed for couples.

I want to be in Kabul with my friends and colleagues to join with them at their conference, to celebrate the realization of a goal we could only dream about in earlier years. I admit to myself that I am afraid to go back to Afghanistan now. I am afraid of the Taliban, which has threatened Loya Jirga delegates with death. Still, the importance of this moment, when women from all over Afghanistan will come together in public to discuss government policy, takes precedence over my fears, and on the last day of November 2003, I leave Washington to begin my third trip to Afghanistan. Judy Lerner, an old friend from Women Strike for Peace, is going with me. At eighty-two, Judy is extraordinary—ebullient, beautiful, intelligent. She sparkles with fun and laughter. During a lifetime of teaching in New York City public schools, she was a leader in the teacher's union and engaged in a host of other activities. Judy is retired, a great-grandmother, and a UN NGO peace advocate. I am very pleased she is going with me.

From the start, the trip is full of small crises. We meet at Kennedy Airport at 5:00 p.m., far too early for a 9:45 departure, so we sit down for a leisurely chat and a cup of coffee, then amble to the departure gate, where we discover the gate was changed. We dash, as fast as two elderly women can, for a cart to drive us to Terminal 8. We are the last to board the plane.

More drama awaits after we arrive at Connie Borde's apartment in Paris. Connie finds out that Judy is traveling with an expired visa to Afghanistan and has been advised to renew it when we get there. Connie will have none of it. After frantic calls to the Afghan embassy in Paris, and trips back and forth in taxis, that problem is finally solved and Judy and I get back to Connie's just before we have to leave for the airport. Let this not be an omen, I think.

At the airport we meet two American expats, Jacqui Duclos and Jane Donaldson, friends of Connie with no previous connection to NEGAR, who are going to Kabul for the Loya Jirga.

Our stopover is Dubai, one of the United Arab Emirates. As we wander around the empty airport after midnight, waiting for our flight to Kabul, Judy and I bond with Jacqui. Her height and gorgeous mane of blond hair are dramatic; she has a great sense of fun, is very smart, and even more compelling to me, she is a seeker and doer. She was active in Students for a Democratic Society during college in the 1960s, and after graduation went to France, where she has lived and worked for over thirty years. She tells us about the months she lived and studied in a Nepalese monastery with a Buddhist master, where she became a practicing Buddhist, though she still retains a strong Jewish identity.

We board the plane for Kabul, and my sense of trepidation takes over once again. I think back to my first arrival at Kabul's airport more than thirteen years ago, when the plane was forced to make a spiraling descent to elude mujahidin missiles aimed at the city. I remember the silence of the shabby airport when Gabi, Cynthia, and I landed. I also flash back to our frenzied departure, when Shakira and Zahera literally pushed us onto the plane through the crowds desperate to leave the doomed city.

When we land, the small airport is just as I remember it. There is a mob of people, pushing and shoving, just as when we left in 1990. But these Afghans are shouting happily, eager to greet waiting family and friends. I see Zubair and then Nasrine, who runs up to us. Everyone seems entangled, arms embracing, backs and shoulders butting. Nasrine is everywhere, collecting conference guests, exhorting and demanding efficiency from the airport officials, instructing NEGAR volunteers and drivers to gather us and our baggage onto transportation to the city.

I am totally bewildered as we drive through Kabul to our hotel. I had envisioned terrible destruction from the mujahidin civil war, the Taliban rule, and American bombs. Instead, I find a city that has seemingly gotten over all that and gone wild with construction. Scaffolding and new buildings are rising everywhere. There was hardly any traffic in Kabul in 1990; now, hordes of yellow Toyota taxis jam the streets, along with private vehicles of every description and function.

The NEGAR women have arranged for us to stay in one of the many small hotels that are springing up overnight, this one the Insaf Hotel on busy Charahi Ansari Street. As soon as I walk through the lobby and up the flight of stairs to the second-floor rooms, the acrid odor of drying concrete and the vapor of fresh paint and shellac take me back twenty years, to a room in Nairobi, in one of the units expeditiously constructed for delegates to the UN World Conference on Women. The smell may be the same, but the room in Nairobi was far better than the one here. Nairobi in 1985 was a modern city far more advanced economically and technologically than Kabul today.

But we are fortunate to have a new, clean room with two narrow cots and a tiny bathroom. One florescent light gives uncertain illumination, and central heat being virtually unknown in Kabul, a gas heater is brought into our room along with a bulky gas tank. The heater rapidly warms the small room but the fumes are powerful; with inoperable windows and no ventilation, we keep the gas on only intermittently.

I am especially delighted to see Zubair again. Earlier this year, as a token gesture of thanks for his great help in getting me out of Khoja Bahauddin, I had invited him, his wife, Manija, and baby daughter, Zainab, to stay with me in Washington for three months to study English. It had been a challenging period for all of us, but I believe it was a great learning period for them. I certainly learned a great deal from them, including his account of growing up in Kabul during the Communist period and how he had evaded the Taliban to join Massoud.

Now, in Kabul, it is nearly eight months since they left Washington. He and Manija have a new baby girl, so their visit was also productive in another way. Zubair had been working for the Foreign Ministry when they came to visit, but now he has taken a leave, hoping to find work that will pay better. He plans to be with me every day while I'm here and has arranged for a car and driver. But for this, our first day in Kabul, Judy and I prefer to walk. So Zubair leads us out into the city. It is difficult to do much talking as we walk, since the broken sidewalks and construction debris require us to watch our step and often to walk single file.

"What is that new building going to be?" I shout back to Zubair, pointing to a tall building with immense panes of blue glass going up a few blocks from the hotel. He shrugs. "I have no idea, maybe offices, maybe stores. Some rich returning Afghan is building it. He hasn't announced what it's for."

"What will be constructed here?" I ask, pointing to a deep excavation ready to become the foundation for another large building. Zubair shrugs again. "I don't know. Maybe a government building, maybe stores. No one knows."

The interim government's first imperative is to rebuild essential institutions and infrastructure. It has neither time nor funds to undertake planning and even lacks the bureaucratic ability to oversee new construction. Entrepreneurial Afghans are simply moving ahead on their own. We walk past shops started up in old bullet-scarred, crumbling buildings, some so decrepit they seem ready to collapse.

Soon it is time to turn back. Dinner and a meeting with Nasrine and Shoukria has been called for 6:00 p.m. at Popo Lano, a popular Italian restaurant next door to our hotel. The décor is simply amazing: on the lower walls, there are alternating panels of dark wood, white plaster embossed with vines, and mirrors painted with flowers. Above these panels, gold-framed oil paintings hang between white fluted columns. The ceiling is awash in pink, green, and yellow painted flowers. On the center wall, backed by a huge gold-framed mirror, is a gilded altarpiece. Several of us debate whether this fantastic decor is based on old Afghan motifs such as the white marble mausoleum of Queen Gawharshad (1377-1457), with its intricate carvings and stucco dome of lapis blue, brick red, gold, and white, or on the riotously painted trucks of the Kuchi, the Afghan gypsies. In any case, I love its exuberance and color, a flagrant reaction to the puritanical Taliban ethos.

About twenty French and American women and men are assembled at two tables. It is a convivial gathering, minus drinks or wine, since this is still a Muslim country. Nasrine arrives nearly two hours after the rest of us, Shoukria a little later. They have been dealing with last minute details for the meeting, and both look exhausted. Shoukria speaks in French and Nasrine translates for the Americans, describing their mutual fears about Taliban terrorism and disruption.

"The Taliban is back," Shoukria says, "but the important truth is that the Taliban is not back like it was before. They are getting asylum and support from our neighbors again. But they no longer have the use of Pakistan's air force or Pakistan's overt commitment of military reinforcements."

Shoukria also wants to be sure that we recognize that even though women will be at the Loya Jirga, which is progress, "there are some who want women to have complete equality, while others operate out of fear and want less." But tomorrow she tells us, two thousand women from provinces throughout Afghanistan will come together to discuss how to guarantee their rights. I am deeply skeptical that anywhere near that number can be brought together. It would be a triumph if several hundred women, defying threats and pressure, meet in Kabul tomorrow.

The next morning Zubair fills the car with me and Judy and our new friends, Jacqui and Jane, and we are driven to the Park Cinema, where the conference will take place. We are stunned by the sight of hundreds of women streaming past us into the theater. The huge auditorium is packed, and the balcony likewise overflows with women. Considering that for five years under the Taliban the women of Kabul have been invisible, it is incredible that Shoukria was right; nearly two thousand women, not one of whom is hidden under a burqa, have come together in a public venue. We are told that more women have been turned away for lack of space.

Foreign guests are seated in the front rows. I squeeze in close to my friends on deeply cushioned sofas. It is freezing, much colder than outside, where the sun is shining. We keep on our heavy coats, scarves, and gloves. The cavernous auditorium is dim despite some electric lights and a row of tall stained-glass windows of arabesque design. The electricity goes off periodically, plunging the hall into pitch blackness. But the women laugh and continue talking. I keep jumping up to look at the sea of faces extending way to the back of the auditorium and up to the balcony. I marvel that Shoukria, Nasrine, and the women of NEGAR have pulled all this together with so few resources and despite threats from the Taliban.

Along the walls, hanging from the balcony, and backing the stage are long banners. They are in Dari, French, and English. The stage backdrop has a large replica of NEGAR's logo and in Dari and English reads: "NEGAR: SUPPORT OF WOMEN OF AFGHANISTAN—3 Day Conference of Kabul/December 4, 5, 6, 2003—Peace, Constitution, and the Declaration of the Essential Rights of Afghan Women."

Another banner announces: "After Long Years of War and the Darkness of the Taliban, The Peace Process, the Constitution and Elections Are a Date with History of the New Afghanistan." Yet another claims: "The Constitution Must Eternalize the Inalienable and Equal Rights of Men and Women of Afghanistan."

On this, the opening day, there are a handful of men sitting up front, along with notables who will address the meeting. There has never been, in the millennial history of Afghanistan, such a gathering of women—informed, articulate, and determined to be a legitimate part of the constitutional process. The spirit in the hall is so strong that the walls seem to reverberate with the fervency of their hopes.

The meeting opens with a prayer intoned by an elderly

woman, instead of the traditional mullah. Shoukria, Nasrine, other NEGAR leaders, and the speakers are lined up on the stage. Kabuli women alternate as chairs of the conference. Nasrine translates everything into English. The most important official to speak is Deputy Chief Justice Fazel Ahmad Manawi of the Supreme Court. He is a dynamic speaker and the women respond with delighted laughter and frequent applause.

"Women are the most important group in society," he begins, "because all education begins with mothers. Islam began in an era when all societies discriminated against women; therefore, in declaring the rights of women, the teachings of Islam were in advance of society. It follows that since Islam gives both men and women responsibilities in society, both men and women should have rights in society." Justice Manawi says that he is against women being considered a commodity. Taking a swipe at the West, he adds, "I deplore modern societies' use of women's bodies in advertising."

Manawi is considered the most liberal member of the Supreme Court and is putting forth a somewhat radical vision. Still, it makes me uncomfortable that his speech is entirely within the context of Islamic law, or sharia. The draft constitution states that members of the Supreme Court "should have higher education in law or in Islamic jurisprudence," but I know that neither Manawi nor any of the other nine justices attended any secular law school. The draft constitution also states, "The Supreme Court shall have the authority of the interpretation of the Constitution, laws, and legislative decrees." If the Supreme Court judges are only trained in sharia law, can there be a separation of religion and government, and if not, can sharia really offer women equal rights?

Another speaker that first day is Dr. Massouda Jalal, the first female presidential candidate in the history of Afghanistan. There are some reservations about Dr. Jalal, since she never signed NEGAR's petition for women's rights. She is not a strong speaker, but her analysis of the role a woman could play as president is interesting. She points out that since women had no part in the disastrous conflicts that left Afghanistan in ruins, she, as a woman, can play a crucial mediating role. She gets a warm response from some of the audience, but I also see many shrugs and frowns that suggest deep skepticism that a woman can be president. Before Dr. Jalal leaves, Connie arranges for some of us to meet her for dinner the next evening.

The conference breaks for lunch, served outside in a huge tent-like structure. Temporary fences screen the area from pedestrians. All the fabrics covering the area are richly colored or are silk-screened with gold fleur-de-lis and brilliant red and blue Islamic wheels. Inside the tent, long tables are lavishly spread with platters of nan, cooked meats, salads, and vegetables, plus cans of soft drinks.

The young male waiters are a pleasure to watch as they balance oversized trays above their heads and gracefully slide in and around the hundreds of women eating and conferring. With masterful efficiency, they clear the tables of enormous messes of food, platters, cutlery, and cans and carry it all around a corner to the back of the building. I follow them, intrigued by their skill. Huge caldrons are being sluiced down; enormous platters are scraped, and a rising mound of discarded food and trash lies at the far back. A small girl has found her way through all the fencing and is rapidly piling food into a bag, while other poor children watch from the other side of the fence.

The afternoon speakers talk in Dari, and since neither Nasrine nor anyone else is translating the session, most of the Westerners are frustrated and bored, but I am so engrossed by the women attending the conference that I don't really mind. Most are fairly young, with few past fifty. They are animated, laughing and talking to each other, and they are interested in and responsive to the speakers. It is hard to reconcile these women with the images from the terrible Taliban years of silent figures hurrying through the streets hoping not to be caught in some infraction.

Most of the women have a head covering of some sort. There are many white scarves—gauze, lace, silk, or cotton. Others are patterned, or multicolored knits. There are some uniformed army women with regulation hats. Jacqui and I, wandering through the building with Zubair, come across a group of Hazara village women in the balcony. They are from an ethnic group that has been treated as second class for decades. Except for the two youngest, who wear simple scarves, the women wear burqas that are open in front to reveal their faces or thrown completely back, with their hair uncovered and the cloth trailing down their backs. Along with the usual blue burqas, there are a polka dotted and a paisley one.

"Why are you here?" we ask them.

"We heard about the meeting in a town near us," one of them answers. "We are eager to learn and we came."

"Did your husbands try to stop you?"

"No," another replies. "They were happy that we wanted to go."

"Do you think things will be better now?"

They turn to look at each other, before answering. "We don't know," several answer, "but probably not. It's not easy for change to happen."

We ask their ages and tell them ours. They are not surprised at how well we look for our age compared to women in Afghanistan since, as they tartly point out, "in Afghanistan, we live very hard lives, not like you from the West." These isolated village women want change, education, a better life. They are realistic, skeptical, and determined. I doubt they will ever lie down passively, like sheep to the slaughter.

In late afternoon, Zubair and I leave to drive around the city. I want to drive past some of the landmarks of my 1990 trip. I want to recapture that time and put this visit in context. It is slow going, the dense traffic being completely chaotic. Zubair explains that there are seventy thousand taxis in Kabul, all yellow Toyotas designed to be driven on the left side of the road, while everyone in Afghanistan drives on the right. They were given to the Taliban by Pakistan. Along with the taxis there are bicycles, horse-drawn carts, small buses, and huge trucks that carry goods over long distances. Public transportation has yet to be implemented. Local tradesmen seem to rely on clumsy pushcarts, most often loaded high with market goods. With no traffic lights, each vehicle forces its way ahead, honking relentlessly. Men, women, and children of all ages dart into traffic to get across the road, some of them hauling backbreaking sacks. There are few sidewalks. The pollution is terrible.

Jockeying for position in one such traffic jam, Zubair suddenly points to a looming construction site. "That's the Kabul Hotel where you stayed," he announces. "It's being remodeled." It looks more like a complete reconstruction than a remodeling job. The low, rambling, yellow stucco structure where we stayed had been shabby but possessed a provincial charm. Built in the early years of the last century, it had been a longtime business and meeting place in the center of town, as well as a favorite venue for social engagements like the elaborate weddings I witnessed there. My favorite spaces at the hotel had been the wondrous, neglected garden and the dim back lobby, with its worn oriental rugs and deeply cushioned sofas, where I'd found quiet and solitude.

I learn that the Aga Khan, the billionaire leader of the Shia Muslim Ismaili community, has bought the Kabul Hotel. Americans of a certain age will remember the Aga Khan's playboy father, Aly Khan, who married the film star Rita Hayworth. The for-profit Aga Khan Fund for Economic Development, which owns more than ninety hotels and lodges in Africa and Central Asia, is planning a five-star hotel that will replace the genteel old building. At least the Aga Khan Trust for Culture, another arm of his large empire, is financing repairs at some of the old mosques, shrines, and courtyard houses hidden in the narrow streets of old Kabul.

I cannot find any of the landmarks I remember. I look in

vain for the circular domes and slender minarets of an old
mosque, the several huge Romanesque government buildings
that had once been palaces, a shimmering white Persian-style
building that had been a sports center with swimming pool and
green park. So much destruction, such rash, precipitous building. Darkness falls, as do my spirits, as we return. I know it is
unreasonable, but what I really want for Kabul—the beloved
city of the Mogul emperor Babur, a city celebrated by poets for
its glorious gardens—is to see it rise again, not only in its own
indigenous beauty but also in terms of the welfare of its people.
I want to see less haste and luxury and commercialism, more
affordable housing and schools and clinics, more parks and play-
grounds.

I have also asked Zubair to help me find Shakira and Zahera,
and Zahera's daughter Leila, who would now be 19. I surmise
that some government agency may have records of pre-Afghan
organizations but Zubair says that all agencies are understaffed
and in disarray so we're unlikely to find anyone to help us. He
promises, however, to speak to an official he knows. Several
days later I have depressing news: Zubair reports back that all
records were destroyed either during the civil war or under the
Taliban. He does not know how to proceed further in finding
Shakira and Zahera. I too am at a loss as to how else to look for
my friends, and so the search ends there.

The next days of the conference are its heart and soul, the
reason all these women have come together. Reports from the
ten regional meetings held in the summer and fall are going to
be presented for discussion and affirmation.

In early August NEGAR had held a kick-off meeting in
Kabul to launch the effort to educate provincial women about
the draft constitution and their right to participate. It began
with a ceremonial presentation to the Constitutional Commis-
sion of one hundred thousand of our signatures from petitions
brought from Paris and Washington. Another two hundred
thousand signed petitions were kept back for a future event.

Over a three-month period after the kick-off, regional meetings were held in eight towns. NEGAR's original plan called for meetings of one hundred women at each location. Work kits included the Bonn Agreement, charters on women's rights, UN declarations, and relevant parts of Afghanistan's 1964 constitution. Local women leaders and NEGAR members were trained to analyze the draft constitution, to focus on women's rights, education, social policies, and peace. They would help to prepare recommendations and resolutions for the Kabul conference.

It did not happen quite that way. At the first seminar in Charikar, two hundred and fifty women and fifty men, including the governor of Parwan province, showed up instead of the one hundred women who had been invited. The meeting was so well received that the governor, then and there, created one hundred and four civic posts for women at the provincial level. The numbers kept growing at each regional meeting. NEGAR had underestimated the magnitude of women's eagerness to participate in society and the generally positive response and involvement of men, including regional leaders.

Now, as women present reports from these regional meetings, the women in the hall are electrified, applauding and waving their arms for every vote. The conference is moving and exhilarating. Yet I am still gloomy. NEGAR's great work has created space for women's energies, capabilities, and aspirations, a space that will hopefully allow them to be a part of building the future. My sadness stems from a sense of how fragile it all is. Rumors are circulating that the Loya Jirga is going to be postponed; there is gossip that leaders within Massoud's faction of the Northern Alliance are moving away from each other, and worst of all, that the Taliban is gaining strength and moving up toward Kabul.

I also realize, once again, that what happens to Afghanistan is not just about Afghanistan. It seems to me that there is a kind of universal, inchoate disorder affecting all nations. Never before have I thought in terms of Good and Evil, but I wonder now if the astounding rise of extremism among many religions of the world is a consequence of some perilous conjuncture we cannot yet comprehend. The notion that it is not just Afghanistan, but humanity, that is in crisis casts a shadow over my mind.

Leaning closer to Jacqui, I whisper, as if she can read my mind, "Do the bad always win? What is the answer?" She smiles and is silent. Soon she passes me a folded note. I unfold the paper. "The answer is blowing in the wind," it says. Ah, well . . .

That evening, a small group of us join Massouda Jalal, the presidential candidate, for dinner at the Hotel Intercontinental. Dr. Jalal, a pediatrician and lecturer in medicine at Kabul University, has brought along her husband, a professor of law at the university. Dr. Jalal is soft-spoken; a slight smile plays on her pale, perfectly oval face. In contrast to her husband, who pro- jects nervous energy, there is an almost Buddha-like quality to her.

We ask Dr. Jalal again why she is running. "It is very important for women to stand up and demand a place among the policy-makers," she replies. Repeating her speech at the conference, she continues, "Never before in the five-thousand-year history of Afghanistan have women participated in political power. I accept that historic challenge." Everyone nods approval. "You know that I have challenged Karzai once before? And with some success," she adds. We did not know this.

"During the emergency Loya Jirga, immediately after the fall of the Taliban, I challenged Karzai for the position of interim president. I came in second with over 170 votes. Karzai offered me a position as his deputy if I would withdraw, but I wanted to challenge, whether I won or not."

We are impressed; none of us other than Connie had realized that Dr. Jalal had run for office and done so well. But when Dr. Jalal begins to speak disparagingly of the Northern Alliance and condemns Karzai for appointing Northern Alliance leaders to his cabinet, I decide to liven things up a bit.

"Well, you know, I wouldn't disparage the Northern Alliance so roundly," I say. "They were, I recall, the only group defending Afghanistan against the Pakistan invasion via the Taliban!"

Professor Jalal abruptly sits up. "These are dangerous men, undemocratic, warlords! They destroyed Kabul," he growls.

"Weren't they defending Kabul?" I answer. "I thought the great Ahmad Shah Massoud, whose photograph is all over Kabul, was saving the city and the people from the fundamentalist Hekmatyar."

Angry with me, fiercely defensive of his wife, the professor seems to dislike a challenge from any other woman. Connie also disapproves of my provocation. Clearly, just because my friends support the Northern Alliance doesn't mean that other Afghans don't have valid concerns about them. Of course, I know that people of goodwill experience similar events in completely different ways; it's just that sometimes it's hard for me to admit it.

Dr. Jalal and her husband did not go into exile either during the Soviet war or during the rule of the Taliban. In fact, she was one of the few women allowed to work under the Taliban, directing an all-women's project within the World Food Programme. Despite finding the couple stiff and cold, I admire Dr. Jalal's tenacity and her husband's fierce loyalty to her.

The purpose of the last day of the conference is to identify items that the regional women want included in the new constitution. These create a fascinating picture of the kind of society the women hope for, as well as the challenges they face in getting there. The resulting list includes several recommendations specifically concerning human rights:

> Implementation of international human rights charters and
>   other agreements to which the nation is a signatory
> The expression "women's rights" to be included specifically,

rather than assumed to be included, within the general
term "citizens rights"

Then there are items that reflect the specific life conditions of
Afghan women:

Establishment of laws preventing girls from being given
away or sold to pay for a crime or to solve a dispute
between families
The right of women to sing the national anthem—in
either Dari or Pashto
Identity cards issued at birth for women as well as men
Freedom from being told what to wear and the right to
participate in sports and cultural life
A review of the 1964 and 1977 constitutions to adopt
specific provisions that were beneficial to women

There are also "dream" items that have yet to be part of most
national constitutions:

Free health clinics for women and children
Obligatory education through fourteen to fifteen
years of age
Free education through university
Parliament to have 30 percent women members

The women raise points that address their hatred of the
Taliban and the "Arabs" who came into Afghanistan with the
Taliban. All foreigners with the Taliban and Al Qaeda are called
"Arabs" by Afghans, and the fact that they were given Afghan
names and identity cards by the Taliban is still an issue. The
women demand that those identity cards be revoked. But there
is debate about children conceived by rape or forced marriage of
Afghan women to the so-called Arabs. In Afghanistan the line
of descent is patrilineal; hence these children are not Afghans
and have no civil rights. This, in turn, means that the Afghan

women living outside the country in refugee camps who have borne these children cannot bring them across the border into Afghanistan. The women vote to restore the identity and rights of the children. (The Loya Jirga later votes to deny these children citizenship, despite eloquent arguments presented by both Nasrine and Dr. Jalal.)

When the conference ends, Judy and I plan to spend a few days socializing and touring the city. We visit Mary MacMakin's new PARSA center, with living quarters for her and guests, a women's workshop, and a sales room for their products. There is also a garden for growing vegetables, dormant now for the winter. It is abundantly clear that Mary has happily settled in for the long term and we soon leave as another group of Western women arrive to see her.

We also go to a dinner party at the new home of a NEGAR activist. Leaving our shoes in the entryway, we enter a spacious living room, where at least fifty Afghan women are sitting on the floor, leaning on cushions and against the walls. A few have brought babies. The red wall-to-wall carpeting is overlaid with a white Chinese rug. Champagne-colored velvet drapes cover the windows and a gas stove is beside one wall, yet the room is chilly enough for everyone to wear a sweater or silk padded jacket. After much eating and conversation, a group of women in the corner pick up large brass trays and begin a rhythmic drumbeat. Our beautiful hostess leads off with a swaying dance. Her long blue-patterned velvet robe catches the light as she moves her body to the beat. She moves away from the center, another woman rises to perform, and the women begin to clap in rhythm. Judy jumps up, throws her arms in the air, and with a big grin performs a relatively sedate bump and grind. The women love it.

Jacqui and Jane are leaving for Paris on Sunday afternoon, so Zubair takes us all shopping for gifts in the morning. We park near the Kabul River, which after years of drought is now barely an ebbing stream. Small vendors have set up their wares on the dry, rocky riverbed, near the concrete embankment that formerly confined the river. Above, the embankment walls are covered with brilliant crimson carpets for sale; their owners lounge on the wall waiting for buyers, their shoes neatly deposited on the ground. It is a warm, sunny day and almost all the men wear their traditional shalwar kameez, some with light suit jackets over the long tunic. I see very few beards or turbans. The women wear long skirts; most have shawls over their heads or wrapped around their shoulders. Many women still wear their burqas, but most keep their faces uncovered and their hands free. They also reveal their skirts, shoes, and handbags—the sight of which had been forbidden by the Taliban. Men crowd around money changers. Mounds of huge cauliflowers and piles of green beans, carrots, potatoes, cabbages, legumes, onions, and turnips are heaped on carts or spread on the ground. The vegetables rival any in the world.

After Jacqui and Jane's departure, Judy and I decide to move to the Intercontinental Hotel, as both of us have had enough of the fumes from the gas heaters. We have to pass through heavy security before gaining entrance and realize that we will be overlooking the arrangements for the Loya Jirga, which will take place directly below the hotel.

That evening we go to Zubair's house for dinner. I am eager to see Zainab, his two-year-old daughter who was with Zubair and Manija in Washington. Zubair and his family live on the first floor of a rented house with his old father. The second story is occupied by his middle brother, a policeman, and the brother's wife and eight children. I have no sense of where we are as we drive through the dark, quiet city. High walls on either side of the passing streets create a mysterious atmosphere. As we drive into their small compound, Zubair's oldest brother, who will represent the family, comes out with a flashlight to guide us inside. Shoes off in the entry, curtains pulled aside, and we enter the main room, lit by a flickering, battery-charged electric lamp. Later, a brighter electric light comes on. Most houses in Kabul have their own, frequently unreliable, generators.

Large tapestries of Massoud hang on two walls; the others are covered with coarse lace curtains embellished with red satin drapes and swags. Cushions are already piled up for me to sit on. The ninety-four-year old father sits silently, cross-legged, on the floor. The oldest brother sits beside Judy and me. He lives elsewhere with his six sons and has brought along the youngest, about two years old, with whom he gently plays. This brother runs the Kabul airport and will soon open an Arianna Airlines office in Frankfurt. He speaks English, but our conversation is forced and formal. Zubair brings Zainab in but she is too shy to come to me. Manija carries the baby, quite as beautiful as Zainab. The baby's eyes are outlined with kohl. Manija seems tired and faded.

I embrace her. "How are you? I am so happy to see your new baby." She bows her head, smiles, and nods, but doesn't speak, even though she spent many weeks learning English in the States. "Manija," I scold, "you speak English! Are you continuing your studies? The baby is beautiful and I know it's hard taking care of both of them, but I hope you are taking time to study." She smiles with lowered head, but again says nothing.

"She doesn't have time," Zubair breaks in. Manija takes Zainab's hand and leaves the room with the children. Zubair follows her. I attempt conversation with the brother until Zubair and Manjia come back with large trays, which are put on the floor before us. Manija has cooked my favorite vegetable dish, one that she frequently made in Washington, cauliflower and eggplant stewed with onions and tomatoes. There are also meat patties, rice and nan, and a platter of beautifully cut and arranged vegetables. Manija leaves the room as soon as the food is served, which saddens me. I realized during their time living with me that she had fully internalized aspects of her traditional upbringing, and she was unlikely to break out of the mold that defined so many Afghan women. But I cannot help being disturbed that she did not see this evening as a public occasion in which she could participate. Her submissive manner, lowered head and eyes, sadden me. I am angry that Zubair has not aggressively helped Manija continue her English lessons and insisted that she have a position of equality in the family. I remind myself that I do not know the real family dynamics. I do know that Zubair is worried about his future, still searching for his place and path in this fragile, troubled country.

But I also feel badly about my own role during the evening. I wish I had asked that Zainab be kept in the room to slowly ease her shyness with me. I could have insisted that Manija also stay in the room and eat with us—or would that have increased everyone's discomfort? Tired and frustrated, I ask Zubair to take us back to the hotel early. In any case, we are going to leave in the morning for the Panjshir Valley and have to pack for a possible overnight stay.

In the morning, sunlight floods the elegant dining room of the Intercontinental; the buffet is lavish, full of Western-style foods that I have been missing, but I am feeling queasy and keep to oatmeal, toast, and tea. Zubair and our driver arrive. We leave to rendezvous with a carload of American friends of Nasrine and then set off for the famous seventy-mile-long valley, deep in the Hindu Kush mountains, that was Massoud's base and beloved home.

The valley is approximately sixty miles northeast of Kabul. The Soviets launched six major expeditions against Panjshir between 1980 and 1982 because of the valley's proximity to the Salang Highway, which cut through the mountain range and was the only reliable overland supply route to Kabul. Thousands of Soviet soldiers were killed defending Salang against Massoud's mujahidin. In the fall of 1982, the Soviets sent ten thousand of their troops, along with four thousand of the Afghan Communist government's troops and scores of tanks, attack helicopters, and fighter jets, into the valley. More than 80 percent of Panjshir's buildings were damaged or destroyed, crops were ruined, and livestock were killed. The people of the valley suffered unimaginable hardships. In the spring of 1983, Massoud declared a truce and the Soviets agreed to stop attacking the Panjshir, while Massoud agreed to let the Communist government operate an army base at the southern end of the valley around Salang.

The following spring, Massoud learned that the Soviets planned another assault, the largest yet, including a week of aerial bombing followed by an avalanche of land mines. Massoud led more than forty thousand Panjshiris into hiding in the mountains. The Soviet troops entered a deserted valley, and Massoud's commandos continued fighting from rugged mountain caves. Even the Soviet generals admired his mastery of guerrilla warfare, and the Panjshir Valley became a symbol of the ultimately unconquerable nature of Afghanistan.

It is a beautiful warm December day as we head out of Kabul on a paved road. Little white flags flutter alongside the road, extending back into the barren land. I ask Zubair about them, and he explains that they signal unexploded land mines. Statistics come to life as we look at the white flags so close to the road. Afghanistan remains one of the world's most mined countries, with millions of explosives laid over the past twenty-three years by Soviets, mujahidin, and the Taliban. Between 15 and 20 percent of all farmland is mined, in a country where agriculture has always been the predominant economic activity. Land mines not only are an obstacle to reconstruction, but also continue to kill and maim farmers and their children.

All along the roadside are shacks crammed with things for sale—fresh, canned, or bottled foods, fabrics, mechanical parts, all piled haphazardly. Some of the shacks are domiciles as well. Women in padded, patchwork cotton jackets, traditional baggy pants, and headscarves sit beside their wares, waiting for someone to stop.

I ask Zubair if we will pass through the Shomali Plains, once one of the most fertile regions in the country, on our way to Panjshir. "But we are on the Shomali Plains now!" he exclaims.

"I know there was a lot of fighting here," I say, horrified, "and crops were destroyed, but all those vineyards and orchards and villages—they just can't have been totally wiped out." "The Taliban and Al Qaeda had a scorched-earth policy here," Zubair says. "They made everyone leave. About two hundred thousand people were forced off their land. The Taliban poisoned water wells and blew up ancient irrigation systems and grapevines and burned them so they could never be replanted. They torched walnut trees. Houses, shops, all buildings were burned to the ground." Millions of Afghan farming and village families were uprooted, and driving through the barren landscape makes it more real than any of the stories I have heard.

It is hard to imagine that this land was once fragrant with flowers and bountiful with fruit and grain. Some 80 percent of Afghanistan's rural population traditionally owned the land they lived and worked on, and as a consequence of living in one of the harshest environments on earth, they were scrupulous stewards of their family legacies. For over fifteen centuries, Afghan peasants, predating those in China, used their horizontal-vaned windmills for power. Villagers solved the problem of evaporation from open-air canals by digging underground irrigation systems, which went as deep as one hundred twenty feet below the surface and extended as far as twenty miles. Vertical shafts every one hundred yards or so were maintained by teams to repair cave-ins and clear out debris.

"But why would they destroy the grapevines and orchards?" Judy asks. "This was their own land, the same as the fields they had grown up on. How could Afghans do this to their own land, to their own people?"

This is history I know, so I answer before Zubair can. "The Afghan refugees who wound up in Pakistan madrassas were Pashtun, from the south. The Afghans who lived here were Tajiks. And everybody was fanning ethnic hatred: The Pashtuns who led the Taliban, the Pakistan Wahhabi madrassas where the boys were taught, the Saudi money that funded the

Al Qaeda camps and soldiers. So to Pashtun youth, the Tajiks were no longer their people."

Zubair agrees with me, but adds, "Anyway, the leaders of the Taliban militias are Arabs, not Afghans, not the kids from the madrassas. The militants are Chechen, Uzbek, Pakistani." Of course, I know that many if not most of the leaders of the Taliban are Afghans, but I remain silent out of consideration for Zubair.

The tarmac road continues for about thirty miles before it is replaced by rough dirt roads. The mountains appear in the distance, blue, with snow glinting off the high peaks. Soon enough we are driving through them. The air is colder but intensely clear and invigorating. At an open field, we pass hundreds of heavy war machines lined up in perfect rows. I see more tanks than I can count, Scud missiles, multiple-barrel rocket launchers, and much else. These are Northern Alliance armaments that General Fahim, director of the Defense Ministry, has said he will move into Kabul and turn over to the Karzai government. A few days after we leave the valley, prior to the convening of the Loya Jirga, the weaponry is moved. It is a dramatic statement to demonstrate that the Tajik minister of defense and his faction will not disrupt the delicate task of nation building. None of the other warlords will follow his example—not the Pashtuns along the borders with Pakistan; or Rashid Dostum, the Uzbek commander of Mazar-i-Sharif; or Ismail Khan, commander of Herat, the celebrated city of beauty and culture close to the Iranian border.

Further into the valley, our driver stops before a shabby building in a roadside cluster of wooden houses. We are ready for lunch. Inside are rough wooden tables but I want to sit on a rickety balcony I spy on the side. It hangs over a rushing stream, which leaps and burbles as it descends down the rocky hill. I clumsily drop down to the floor and lean against the side of the shack. Everyone is stimulated by the cold air, the towering mountains, the streams of water gushing down the slopes. It is an intoxicating change after all the dryness. I quietly write in my journal while the others walk and climb wooded trails and return for grilled meat kabobs.

We drive on through a narrow dirt road, which is the pass through the mountains into the broad valley. There are steep, ragged ridges on either side. The road dips down close to the rock-strewn river, then climbs, and then the steep mountains recede and miniature fields and small orchards appear on either side of the river as the valley opens up before us. Both cars suddenly pull over onto the side of a low cliff overlooking the river, and we all jump out while our drivers and Zubair go running down the hill toward several fishermen.

I move slightly apart from the others and stand still, then slowly begin to turn in a circle; I look down to the river, then all around. I take in the whole prospect and am transfixed. I am standing in the midst of one of the most beautiful and historic spots in Afghanistan, something I thought I had forever missed. The Panjshir River, sometimes called the Five Lions River, lies below. The fishermen are casting into a still, deep, dark blue pool. A few yards farther along, the water courses over rocks and boulders; it foams and glitters, turning a lighter, paler blue, then slows, and meanders, winding around islets of waving brown grasses. Around a bend in the river, ringed closely by the rising mountains, we can see a terraced field, above which hangs a cluster of two-story, flat-roofed stone houses. On the opposite bank are trees, finally, after so many, many miles of denuded landscape. It is December, and the deciduous trees are bare, but the spreading tops are already festooned with tiny buds, each tree shimmering with a citrine green crown. It is a great miracle that the land can come alive again, renew itself and be fertile, despite the wartime devastation. All around us rise the snow capped, jagged mountains of the great Hindu Kush. I am filled with awe and happiness.

Zubair and the drivers come running back up the hillside, exclaiming that they have bought a basket of fish that they will cook for dinner that night. The houses here are very different from the mud-brick ones I am used to. In the lowest parts of the valley, the foundations are built of stone; farther up, the entire houses are of stone, made of rounded river boulders chinked with mud plaster. Most houses have two stories. In the winter, farm animals are kept on the ground floor, and their body heat warms the upper floor. Zubair points out larger houses and tells us of their various owners. These include the Massoud family and Dr. Abdullah, the foreign minister whose helicopter flew me out of Afghanistan in 2001.

Once, we pull over while Zubair jumps out to embrace a young man, a cousin, who lives in Kabul but is vacationing at his family house. Zubair's family home here was destroyed by Soviet bombs, but they hope to rebuild soon and use it for summer vacations.

Next we drive through a broad stretch of the valley where the cultivated land extends to the horizon of the encircling, amethyst mountains. Fields are faintly tinged with the new green of early crops. How much more beautiful it must be in the spring, with the orchards blooming, apple and cherry blossoms perfuming the air, drifting petals coloring the ground. It is land such as this that has made the Afghan people so passionate about returning to their homeland. But outside a few places such as this Panjshir Valley, most of the country's millions of refugees will not be coming home to fertile fields and standing homes. In addition to 23 years of brutal warfare and destruction, the worst drought in a century has created desert that is swallowing up villages. Once-rich wetlands have dried into caked beds and the great forests of pistachio, cedar, and conifers have almost disappeared. Much of the magnificent wildlife, which included Siberian cranes, snow leopards, and flamingoes, is now seldom seen.

The sun has disappeared behind a low-hanging dark cloud as we climb to a small plateau, a solitary spot. A simple circular white building sits in the center of the site, its emerald green dome topped by a small Islamic symbol. This is Massoud's tomb, exposed to the elements of the Hindu Kush, a symbol of the preeminent warrior, the Lion of Panjshir. The green national flag of Afghanistan whips in the wind. A billboard picture of Massoud, at a distance from the tomb, shows him sitting cross-legged on a prayer rug wrapped in a large, heavy shawl, pakol cap on his head, holding an open book. Inside the small mausoleum, its marble floor layered with rich carpets, Massoud's black marble sepulcher is covered with a green prayer cloth imprinted with gold calligraphy. We stand in silence, solemn in prayer or thought.

The winds are gusting up and it has grown much colder under a lowering white sky. I ask Judy if she would mind if we drive straight back to Kabul, since I am beginning to feel quite ill. She admits to nausea as well, so we tell Zubair our change of plans. The return will be no problem, but first he has to arrange for the others to spend the night at a Northern Alliance guesthouse. We all drive off as snowflakes tumble and swirl in the now biting wind. An hour later we pull up to a long wall. Zubair gets out and knocks on the wooden gates. Those in the other car go inside, and we drive off. That large compound, like the one at Khoja Bahauddin, had once been full of action, housing visiting mujahidin leaders and allies, humanitarian and aid groups, journalists and others. But few come to the Valley now. Judy and I huddle into our warm coats and fall asleep until we reach Kabul, where I fall into bed and a deep sleep. But I begin to vomit during the night, and in the morning we are both feeling very sick.

At the hotel we watch a CNN report stating that two thousand American troops are being deployed to engage the Taliban. We agree to leave Kabul as soon as we can. Zubair finds out that all flights to Dubai are filled today but there is one tomorrow to Sharjah, one of the seven tiny desert kingdoms that make up the United Arab Emirates, which all together are about the size of Maine. The next morning we are packed and ready to leave early but security for the Loya Jirga has tied up traffic, causing Zubair to be late. We make a dash for the airport but miss the flight by less than five minutes, and will have to wait again for the next day's flight. We decide to go back to the Insaf for the night, so we won't run into problems with the Loya Jirga security again, and we are greeted like returning family.

In the morning we drive to the airport with time to spare, and Judy and I wait in the unkempt terminal lobby while Zubair goes off, presumably to pick up our tickets. He comes back shortly, hesitant, to inform us that the plane to Sharjah is full. Judy and I are devastated. Zubair goes back to see what he can do. And then I vomit all over the dirty marble floor in front of me. People stare and shake their heads, some in sympathy, others in horror at the mess. Humiliated, I take a handful of tissues from Judy and try to clean up the floor and myself. Then I rush outside and throw up again, in front of the building.

Zubair returns and says they can get me a single seat; I tell him I will not go without Judy. "Where is your brother?" I cry out. "We have to get on that plane." Again Zubair leaves. It is 12:45, and the flight is scheduled for 1:00. He returns and tells us, miraculously, that we can board the plane. We grab, carry, pull, and push our bags and run after Zubair, rushing through doors and turnstiles. Then we are stopped. As the minutes tick away, we have to fill out forms. Our bags are taken, forms received, and we run outside as the bus to the plane pulls away with a few late passengers. I shout and want to run after it, but Zubair pulls me back. "It will be back for you," he assures us. And he's right. We kiss him goodbye as the bus returns, board the waiting plane, and slump into two back-row seats as we lift into the sky over Kabul.

As I lie back in the seat, I realize that this is the third time my departure from Afghanistan has been both desperate and comedic. Over the years I have been irresistibly pulled into Afghanistan and ignobly pushed out. In my exhausted and over-wrought state, I feel that Afghanistan and I are bound together in some fated way—nonsense, of course, but a powerful feeling nonetheless. In my heart, I know that this is the last trip I shall ever take to Afghanistan; I fear that if I should return, I may never be able to leave.

It is a short flight, but it is twilight when we land in the coastal emirate. The moisture-filled, tropical air is medicine to our desiccated skin. By the time we are ensconced in a taxi rolling toward Dubai, it is dark, and the brilliant lights of the city's skyscrapers flash across the ebony Persian Gulf as though from another planet after the dense blackness of Kabuli nights.

The following morning we leave on the ten-hour flight to France. We go through security and wait for hours, only to repeat security that evening for the flight to the United States, when the guards ask Judy and me to move away from the plane door just as we are about to board. Several agents set up a table in the bridge between the terminal and the airplane and begin a thorough search, emptying our pocketbooks and our cosmetic bags, unwinding our lipsticks, feeling us up and down. It is cold and Judy and I bitterly complain. The agents shrug and reply that American security asked for this, not the French.

Finally, we are let on the flight. This is the end of my thirteen-year "adventure." And yet, as this last security check shows, it was my country's "adventure" into Afghanistan as well. I know this is just what imperial nations do, have always done—the British did it, the Russians did it, Alexander and Genghis Khan did it, and so it goes on, down through the ages. Men wield their power, not only in the games they play with the geopolitical map, but also in their control of women's bodies and their lives.

But this time in Afghanistan, all these things seem to have taken their most extreme form, and Afghanistan has become the front line for two of the most important issues of this era: saving the earth and bringing women into full equality. Too slowly, but finally, I hope, the world will understand that only when all of humanity's energy and creativity is released, not just that of one-half of humanity, will we be able to save ourselves.

I think of the wonderful women I have met or learned about as their stories have begun to emerge. They have come out from under the veil with accounts of courage and ingenuity. Simple women as well as educated women who had once been leaders, resisted the Taliban and built, sometimes in isolation, in other cases communally, clandestine systems of communication, education, and mutual assistance. A form of Islam that many would consider corrupted traumatized women and children in Afghanistan. But Afghan women have also found solace and strength in a truer Islam. These heroic Muslim women have much to teach us and I look forward to learning from them as I finally acknowledge that I am old and becoming too frail for more robust adventure. As I get ready to disembark in America, I know that Afghanistan will remain my marker to assess humanity's passage through this perilous time.

Afghanistan Chronology

328 B.C.—Alexander the Great [356–323 B.C.] invades region of Afghanistan, founding many cities.

A.D. 664—Muslim conquest of Afghanistan.

997—Mahmud, from Afghan province of Ghazni, invades Punjab, creating first Afghan Empire.

1219—Genghis Khan (1167–1227) the Mongol warrior, invades Eurasia, eastern section of Afghanistan.

1504—Babur, descendant of Genghis Khan, Kublai Khan, and Timur (Tamerlane), captures Kabul, is named King, establishes the Mogol empire in India, and like Kublai Khan and Timur is a great patron of arts architecture.

1747—Ahmad Khan Abdali elected king by tribal council, establishes the last great Afghan Empire, the Durrani.

1809—"The Great Game" between the British and Russian Empires for hegemony over Afghanistan commences. The Treaty of Friendship with Britain is signed whereby Afghan rulers agree to oppose Russian influence.

1837-42—The First Anglo-Afghan war. The British invade Afghanistan, depose the Emir of Kabul.

1878–80—The second Anglo-Afghan war occurs when Britain is unable to control Afghan relations with Russia.

1879—Durrand Line is set by Britain, and becomes the contentious Afghan-Pakistan border.

1919—The third Anglo-Afghan war. Declaration of Afghan independence. Amanullah becomes king, attempts modernization of the country.

1927—King Amanullah abolishes purdah, frees women from the veil, declares universal free education and the end of polygamy; he forms the first elected Afghan Parliament.

1929—Amanullah is forced to abdicate, goes into exile. Nadir Khan becomes king.

1933—Nadir Khan murdered, succeeded by son Zahir Shah, age nineteen, whose uncles rule on his behalf, for thirty years.

1965—Underground Marxist People's Democratic Party of Afghanistan (PDPA) formed, split by two factions, Parcham and Khalq.

1973—Zahir Shah overthrown by his cousin Mohammed Daoud Khan; Afghanistan proclaimed a republic.

1978—PDPA Communist coup, President Daoud killed. PDPA-Khalq President Nur Mohammed Taraki forces land reform, and women's education, which sparks Islamic jihad. Taraki murdered, next PDPA-Khalq President Hafizullah Amin executed.

1979—USSR sends in troops, installs exiled PDPA-Parcham Babrak Karmal as president.

1979–89—Soviet-Afghan war. Pakistan selects seven mujahidin parties for military aid from US and Islamic world to support anti-USSR jihad.

1985—PDPA-Parcham Mohammad Najibullah replaces Karmal as president.

1988—USSR President Gorbachev sets ten-month phased exit. Geneva Accord (USA-USSR) ends outside intervention, allows arms supply.

1989—Soviet troops withdrawn.

1991—Collapse of the Soviet Union.

1992—Mujahidin enter Kabul. Najibullah takes refuge in UN

compound. Burhanuddin Rabbani is the first six-month transitional president of "Islamic State of Afghanistan."

1992—Mujahidin civil war. Kabul destroyed. Country destabilized.

1994—Taliban militias enter from Pakistan, conquer Kandahar.

1996—Taliban enters Kabul. Ahmad Shah Massoud withdraws. Taliban torture and kill Najibullah.

1997—Pakistan, Saudi Arabia, and UAE recognize Taliban government.

1997—Opposition forms government under Rabbani, keeps UN Afghan seat. Massoud leads military resistance with Northern Alliance coalition.

1998—Bin Ladin and Al Qaeda join forces with Taliban leader Mullah Omar.

1998—US embassies in Kenya and Tanzania attacked by Al Qaeda.

2000—USS *Cole* battleship bombed by Al Qaeda in Yemen.

2001—Massoud assassinated. World Trade Center and Pentagon attacked by Al Qaeda. US attacks Al Qaeda and Taliban in Afghanistan.

Declaration of the Essential Rights of Afghan Women
Dushanbe, Tajikistan, June 28, 2000

Section I

Considering that the Universal Declaration of Human Rights, as well as the international statements addressing the rights of women listed in Section II of this document, are systematically trampled in Afghanistan today.

Considering that all the rules imposed by the Taliban concerning women are in total opposition to the international conventions cited in Section II of this document.

Considering that torture and inhumane and degrading treatment imposed by the Taliban on women, as active members of society, have put Afghan society in danger.

Considering that the daily violence directed against the women of Afghanistan causes, for each one of them, a state of profound distress.

Considering that, under conditions devoid of their rights, women find themselves and their children in a situation of permanent danger.

Considering that discrimination on the basis of gender, race, religion, ethnicity and language is the source of insults, beatings, stoning and other forms of violence.

Considering that poverty and the lack of freedom of movement pushes women into prostitution, involuntary exile, forced marriages, and the selling and trafficking of their daughters.

Considering the severe and tragic conditions of more than twenty years of war in Afghanistan.

Section II

The Declaration which follows is derived from the following documents:

United Nations Charter
Universal Declaration of Human Rights
International Covenant on Economic, Social and Cultural
    Rights
International Covenant on Civil and Political Rights
Convention on the Rights of the Child
Convention on the Elimination of All Forms of
    Discrimination against Women
Declaration on the Elimination of Violence against
    Women
The Human Rights of Women
The Beijing Declaration
The Afghan Constitution of 1964
The Afghan Constitution of 1977

Section III

The fundamental right of Afghan women, as for all human beings, is life with dignity, which includes the following rights:

1. The right to equality between men and women and the right to the elimination of all forms of discrimination and segregation, based on gender, race or religion.
2. The right to personal safety and to freedom from torture or inhumane or degrading treatment.
3. The right to physical and mental health for women and their children.
4. The right to equal protection under the law.
5. The right to institutional education in all the intellectual and physical disciplines.
6. The right to just and favorable conditions of work.

7. The right to move about freely and independently.
8. The right to freedom of thought, speech, assembly, and political participation.
9. The right to wear or not to wear the chadari (burqa) or the scarf.
10. The right to participate in cultural activities, including theater, music, and sports.

Section IV

This Declaration developed by Afghan women is a statement, affirmation and emphasis of those essential rights that we Afghan women own for ourselves and for all other Afghan women. It is a document that the State of Afghanistan must respect and implement.

This document, at this moment in time, is a draft that, in the course of time, will be amended and completed by Afghan women.

NEGAR Petition: Statement of Support for the Declaration of the Essential Rights of Afghan Women

The most extreme violation of human and political rights in the world has been vigorously pursued in Afghanistan in a reign of terror under the control of the Pakistani-backed Taliban militias.

On June 28, 2000, at the initiative of NEGAR-Support of Women of Afghanistan, a Paris-based Afghan women's association, several hundred Afghan women from all segments of the Afghan nation assembled in Dushanbe, Tajikistan, to draft and promulgate a "Declaration of the Essential Rights of Afghan Women." With this document, the Afghan women affirm and demand for themselves the inalienable rights that had been assured for them by the Constitution of Afghanistan. The Afghan women reject the false assertions of the Taliban militias that these rights are in contradiction with the religion, culture, and traditions of the Afghan society and nation.

For nearly twenty years, life in Afghanistan has been degraded by foreign and civil wars, but since 1994, the regime of the Taliban militias has, by decree, officially taken away from women all rights to education, to work, and to health. Denial of freedom of movement renders Afghan women practically prisoners in their own homes, in the most extreme situation of material and moral destitution.

This statement in support of the Afghan women's Declaration is part of an international campaign by NEGAR-Support of Women of Afghanistan with the goal of five million signatures to be presented to the United Nations by NEGAR and a delegation of Afghans and their worldwide women and men supporters.

Congress, the US Mission to the UN, and other US policymaking entities must support:

1. The integration of this Declaration as a part of the process

for a just, honorable, and durable peace for the legitimate country of Afghanistan for eventual inclusion in the Constitution;

2. Pressure on Pakistan to end its military, political, and financial support which renders the Taliban militias possible;

3. The denial of recognition of the Taliban militias.

History has demonstrated that supremacist and totalitarian regimes such as the Taliban militias maintain themselves in power only if the rest of the world remains silent.

ACKNOWLEDGMENTS

It is not the end I would have hoped, for the story of political changes I witnessed in Afghanistan. From Communist regime to mujahidin victory and civil war, from chaos to Taliban, followed by liberation and high visionary hopes for women in 2003. And now, in 2008, back to Pakistan supported Taliban militias threatening Afghan civil society again. A tragic story. But it is not the end of history. One must hope that the day will come when demagogic imperialist nations will heed the voice of their people as they did not during the massive, worldwide demonstrations against the US war against Iraq which led to a virtual abandon of desperately needed reconstruction help for Afghanistan.

Writing this book has been lonely work. My deepest appreciation and gratitude to my son, Robby, for his sustained enthusiasm and great help during these eighteen years, including his much needed technical support. My thanks also to my friend, Aviva Kempner, for her faith and gracious help. I've leaned on many other friends and they know they have my gratitude. Both Nasrine and her husband, Max Gross, have always been there for me and have helped in so many ways with their deep knowledge of Afghan society and Islam.

My thanks to the new Director of the Feminist Press, Gloria Jacobs, for her editing which sharpened the narrative flow of my book. I also want to thank the founder of The Feminist Press, Florence Howe, for her acceptance of my manuscript and our discussions for restructuring the book. I greatly enjoyed working with the superb editor, Jean Casella, with whom I had many heated discussions, always resolved with mutual understanding.

Barbara Bick
Martha's Vineyard 2008

The Feminist Press at the City University of New York is a nonprofit literary and educational institution dedicated to publishing work by and about women. Our existence is grounded in the knowledge that women's writing has often been absent or underrepresented on bookstore and library shelves and in educational curricula—and that such absences contribute, in turn, to the exclusion of women from the literary canon, from the historical record, and from the public discourse.

The Feminist Press was founded in 1970. In its early decades, The Feminist Press launched the contemporary rediscovery of "lost" American women writers, and went on to diversify its list by publishing significant works by American women writers of color. More recently, the Press's publishing program has focused on international women writers, who remain far less likely to be translated than male writers, and on nonfiction works that explore issues affecting the lives of women around the world.

Founded in an activist spirit, The Feminist Press is currently undertaking initiatives that will bring its books and educational resources to underserved populations, including community colleges, public high schools and middle schools, literacy and ESL programs, and prison education programs. As we move forward into the twenty-first century, we continue to expand our work to respond to women's silences wherever they are found.

For information about events and for a complete catalog of the Press's 300 books, please refer to our web site: www.feministpress.org.